Letters To My Daughter Claire

Letters To My Daughter Claire

Words of love about life, relationships, and faith

JANIS KRISTIANSEN

Xulon Press
2301 Lucien Way #415
Maitland, FL 32751
407.339.4217
www.xulonpress.com

Scripture quotations taken from the English Standard Version (ESV). Copyright © 2001 by Crossway, a publishing ministry of Good News Publishers. Used by permission. All rights reserved.

Scripture quotations taken from the Holy Bible, New International Version (NIV). Copyright © 1973, 1978, 1984, 2011 by Biblica, Inc.™. Used by permission. All rights reserved.

Front Cover Artwork by Claire Kristiansen

Edited by Xulon Press.

Printed in the United States of America.

ISBN-13: 9781545620113

Dedication

edicated to my daughter Claire, the original recipient of this book. You challenged me to grapple with and figure out many of the answers to the questions you were asking, and mothering you helped me put to words the answers for myself. This is what you are holding in your hands now.

Of course, you and I have discussed these subjects at great length over the years. It was my delight and labor of love for me to write over a period of ten years to give you the original manuscript for this book as your surprise high school graduation gift. The joy on your face that day was my reward.

Table of Contents

Introduction

othering is a hot topic, regardless of how you were mothered. If you were mothered well, warm and loving thoughts come to you when you think about your mother.

If you were not mothered well, a whole host of thoughts and emotions may come to your mind, most of them not so good. Regardless of who you are, no one has neutral or casual thoughts and feelings about one's own mother.

Women have different perspectives about motherhood, and adopt many different ways to mother. Many of them are not bad or wrong; they are just different.

My goal for writing this book is to present some topics that come up while we mother girls, and hopefully I'll address them from a healthy, biblical perspective. Some things I would do differently, and many things I didn't do right in my own mothering journey.

Contained in this book are some of the subjects that I taught my daughter, discussed with her and walked through with her over time. I hope these letters will spark a few ideas for you to discuss with your own daughters, if you are raising daughters of your own. There are a few blank pages at the end of the book for you to write your own thoughts to you daughter or to a young girl you may have the opportunity to influence, or maybe you'd like to write to your younger self.

Some of the topics I discuss are daily life, happiness, joy, love, money, life as a woman, our bodies, friendships with women, movies, media, obedience, judging others, boys, choosing a career, the Bible, and God. You know, the biggies of life. I taught my daughter these things over a long period of time, at age appropriate levels, and ultimately how to thoughtfully approach each of them.

If you were not mothered well, I hope the subjects contained herein may benefit you and help you fill the lack and ease the pain that you feel.

If you didn't have a mother and are curious about what that would be like, here is an inside glimpse of what one mother discussed with her daughter as she was growing up.

Regardless of who you are, I hope this book will bring insights and maybe some healing into your life. We women are all someone's daughter.

Janis Kristiansen

Snohomish County, Washington

2017

1.

You Are My Precious Daughter

*T*oday you are sixteen. Happy birthday! What an awesome, smart, bright young woman you have become. I cannot believe that my baby is already that old. I am so happy for you.

Soon you will be of the age when you can have your own driver's license. As I learned from the first two kids who went before you, your life and mine are going to change. No longer will you need rides to and fro from me, and your independence will blossom overnight as your boundaries suddenly increase. It is a hard day for me, but a rite of passage that millions of mothers have gone through before me. I find myself staring at the fact that, with all of its emotions, my active mothering days are numbered, and we will soon relate to one another as adults.

I will always be your mother. No one else can be called that in your life, and it is my deepest honor and blessing to be your mom. Next to being your dad's wife, being the mom to you and the boys gives me deep satisfaction. I find myself with a lot more time on my hands now that you are the only one at home, and I realize that my mothering role is almost done, and I will enter the new stage in life of being empty-nested.

As your mother, I am compelled by a deep need to explain to you life, God, and how the world works. As I was growing up, very little was explained to me. I felt so directionless, simple, and naive, and I suffered from a lack of wisdom or experience from which to draw.

I sometimes over-explain things and repeat explanations until you can recite them back to me word for word, which must irritate you. But it gives me satisfaction to know that you heard what I have said and have been taught what you need to know before you launch. I hope these words will provide love, comfort, direction, counsel, and hope to you.

Proverbs, one of the books in the Bible, has many verses about the simple who are led astray and how they can overcome this. I do not want you kids to suffer for this nor to wonder why we as your parents didn't take the time to teach you what you need to know about life.

God will take you many new and exciting places and I hope through experiences and years, you will take time every day to thank Him from the bottom of your heart for how richly you are loved and how deep and rich His blessings are. Every daughter is loved and precious to the heavenly Father if she has made the choice to belong to Him.

So I'm going to put a few things down in writing so if anything happens to me, it will help you to remember what I have said and know the love behind it. Those of us who have taken the time to write something for someone else have done it for a reason. My reason is my love for you. You are my precious daughter.

"I thank my God in all my remembrance of you" (Philippians 1:3 ESV).

"The Lord will fulfill his purpose for me; your steadfast love, O Lord, endures forever" (Psalm 138:8).

2.

It's All about Choices

When you have a place you call your own and move into the responsibilities of adulthood, my best practical advice for achieving your dreams, fulfilling your desires, and keeping life on track is: simply, clean your kitchen every day.

Living a fulfilling and well-managed life has to start somewhere. Often people ask girls your age, "What do you want to do after you leave high school?" and the girls give big and amazing answers regarding the worlds they want to conquer and the lofty dreams they want to achieve.

But few ever take the time to explain what fills the gap between here and there. Seldom will adults explain the little steps along the way. How do I get from here to there? What are the steps along the way to get to the dream?

Begin by cleaning your kitchen every day.

"This is so boring, so mundane, so trivial, so underneath me," you moan! Dirty dishes breed like rabbits and constantly appear. "Who wants to waste time slaving over the kitchen sink?" you wail.

For years, I went to bed with the dirty dishes piled in the sink and on the counters, and in the morning that's what greeted me when I got up. They smell bad, and it takes twice as long to clean the kitchen the next day or the day after that because the food is now stuck on the dishes. It's no fun being greeted by the smell of dirty dishes and rotting garbage in the garbage can in the kitchen. A dirty kitchen ruins the whole house.

I was not a very good housekeeper when your dad and I got married. I cleaned the kitchen every couple of days or so. So one year for a "New Year's resolution" (which I rarely make) I said I would go to bed every night with a clean kitchen. And I did.

At first, cleaning the kitchen was a drag when I would rather have been sitting on the couch watching TV. Everyone else was sprawled out on the sofa and chairs relaxing, or they were outside playing, and I felt like a martyr scraping dirty plates. But I devoted the fifteen or twenty minutes to it every night, and now more than twenty years later, it's a habit. Over time my attitude about this unpleasant but needed daily task changed and I realized that this daily discipline was spilling over into other areas of my life that needed changing.

A lot of life is like this. At first the mundane chore seems like such a joy-killer, but in the long run, it does bring order and joy because of the end result. Cleaning the kitchen, making your bed, exercise, daily prayer and Bible reading, eating a healthy diet, keeping an orderly home, paying bills and taxes, nurturing relationships, being married, working outside the home, mothering, and everything else is made up of small tasks that can seem hard or not very fun at the time, but the small decisions add up. These are the steps between here and there, making the possibility of reaching your dreams closer to reality.

People often comment how much your dad and I have accomplished in our lives, and that we have such a great marriage and have three wonderful kids. This did not just happen because we fell into it or stumbled upon it but because we decided to do the hard work and the mundane chores of life so we could reap the rewards of daily discipline. To repeat an old saying, we have climbed this mountain one step at a time, and now we are enjoying this incredible view and the rewards of obedient and disciplined lives. After thirty years of marriage and raising all you kids, I can confidently say that it is worth it.

It's amazing what else fell into place when I cleaned the kitchen every day. Because when one area of your life is disciplined and you see the results, it spills over into other areas. If you have the daily discipline to clean the kitchen every day, this habit can be applied to many other areas. Over time, that adds up to achieving and reaching your dreams.

It's all about the everyday choices, the one-step-at-a-time choices, and answers the question, "What do you want to do after you leave high school?" I suggest starting on the road of reaching a fulfilled and happy life by cleaning your kitchen every day.

"For the moment all discipline seems painful rather than pleasant, but later it yields the peaceful fruit of righteousness to those who have been trained by it" (Hebrews 12:11).

3

Life Is Daily.

*L*ife is so daily. We have daily routines and work or school schedules that dictate to us what our day will consist of. The commitments and responsibilities of life can make our lives feel very daily.

Life is not one big mountaintop experience with majestic music playing in the background. Life is not an adrenaline high followed by a loud round of applause. Expecting this is fantasy, not reality. These things can happen to us, but that's not where we should expect to live on a daily basis.

A structured routine allows us to accomplish worthy endeavors. It keeps order, sanity, and a manageable pace to life, and keeps us rested and mentally clear. It helps us find the peace of Christ because we can seek Him on a daily basis as part of our routine. Routine is a blessing from God. He is the

God of order. Those who grow up in homes with little or no routine have a lot of difficulty as adults.

The daily choices we make add up. If I were asked if the little choices or the big choices were more impacting and consequential, hands down it would be the little choices.

When we make big choices, we give them lots of thought, prayer, analysis, and time to digest the possible consequences. But small choices are quick, impulsive, and spontaneous. This is far more impacting.

Little choices:

- Daily prayer
- Daily manners
- Daily tone of voice
- Daily decisions of how we will work, where we will go
- Daily screen time
- Daily relationships
- Daily treatment of others
- Daily use of time
- Daily use of money
- Daily diet
- Daily exercise

Big choices:

- Where we will go to college

- Our career
- Who we will marry
- Having children
- Where we will live
- Where we will work
- Investing and handling money
- Mission work
- Buying a car
- Buying a house
- Taking long trips

When it comes to the large choices, we explore internet articles, seek advice from others, pray much, and give them intense focus. For the little choices, we just casually walk along, like we're aimlessly picking wildflowers or window shopping. We often make little choices impulsively, without giving them much analysis or forethought.

I will continue to make small, daily choices where I obey God and act out my faith. We must be doers of the Word, not hearers only. Making impulsive, random decisions is so much easier than working out our faith, staying home when we need to, working when we need to, and being faithful to our tasks before us.

How can we reach our dreams? How can we achieve success in our relationships, our marriage, our career, our family, and communities? By being faithful in daily choices.

We must put more thought into each day, to capture it, to harness it so we can give an account for it at the end of our lives. Any achievements in life were accomplished because people made intentional daily choices to arrive at their goal. They did not make big decisions one day and then achieve their goals immediately after that.

Those who obey God, have bettered themselves, earned college degrees, been gainfully employed, achieved financial success, are in good physical condition, have a successful marriage, have well-behaved children, and who can hold good jobs have made daily decisions to work towards their goals. These good things came from the daily decisions they made, not one big decision on one day, and then ignoring the choice after that.

Your dad and I have a good marriage, now going on three decades. Our successful marriage and devoted parenting are only results of our intentional daily decisions made over a long period of time amidst pain, struggles, heartaches, and deaths. And of course along the way there were points when we wanted to give up because it seemed too hard.

I *daily* decide to obey God, to respect your dad, to humble myself and put God, your dad, our family, and our home as priorities over myself. Your father and I had years of fighting and arguing, tearing each other down with our words and demanding our own selfish ways. When we reached absolute misery after about ten years, we changed after much prayer, marriage seminars and retreats, counseling, reading many books on marriage, and following a few great examples of people we knew. We did this after doing it wrong for so long. We now realize the power of the fact that daily choices add up to destruction or to life.

We are to serve others before ourselves. Some days I would rather not do this! These are not natural choices. I would rather do what I want, go where I want, or do what I prefer at home. I'd rather spend hours reading, do yard work, visit my friends, or go shopping, but instead I am home every day to make dinner and to avail myself to do what needs to be done. Wouldn't we rather be sipping iced tea on a white sandy beach, sitting in a lounge chair in the sun, escaping in a good book?

Some days, the boredom of routine can drag me down, but then I remind myself I am not doing this for entertainment; I am doing this for the results, and the outcome. It's what I should be doing to live a life of obedience to God. I want a long and happy life and a marriage that will go the distance and make it until death do us part.

Self-control and self-restraint, unpopular but necessary, are so important for healthy lives but few want to put these into practice. Our days should start with prayer and Bible reading, seeking the Lord first, and then all these things will be added to us, and will come second.

I'm trying to establish in you a sense of stability and predictability that is necessary as you develop to give you a peaceful, nurturing environment. And to do this, it will be my duty and my delight to give you the gift of a life of routine consisting of love, nurturing, guidance, encouragement and instruction that is very daily.

"Give us each day our daily bread" (Luke 11:3).

"For as the body apart from the spirit is dead, so also faith apart from works is dead" (James 2:26).

"Therefore do not be anxious, saying, 'What shall we eat?' or 'What shall we drink?' or 'What shall we wear?' For the Gentiles seek after all these things, and your heavenly Father knows that you need them all. But seek first the kingdom of God and his righteousness, and all these things will be added to you. Therefore, do not be anxious about tomorrow, for tomorrow will be anxious for itself. Sufficient for the day is its own trouble" (Matthew 6:31-34).

"So teach us to number our days that we may get a heart of wisdom" (Psalm 90:12).

Jesus said "If anyone would come after me, let him deny himself and take up his cross daily and follow me. For whoever would save his life will lose it, but whoever loses his life for my sake will save it. For what does it profit a man if he gains the whole world and loses or forfeits himself?" (Luke 9:23-25).

"For we must all appear before the judgment seat of Christ, that each one may receive what is due for what he has done in the body, whether good or evil" (2 Corinthians 5:10).

4

Caring For Your Body

*O*ne of America's obsessions is the body. As you surf images and articles on the internet or go through the checkout line in any grocery store, you will see how the internet advertisers and magazine publishers suggest you feed it, clothe it, enhance it, decorate it, tuck it, shape it, tan it, and flaunt it. Our society is saturated in an obsession with the body.

The body only stays tight for a very short time, dear girl. And as a woman, you will quickly discover that gravity and possible pregnancies will quickly stretch and sag it. The Bible gives very good foresight when it says that beauty is fleeting. We can spend an hour in front of the mirror in the morning fussing over our bodies and faces, but by the end of the day it is faded and undone— and it only took a day. Add to each day years of gravity, life, pregnancy and childbirth, child rearing, dietary choices, work, levels of exercise, messy relationships, stresses, bills, taxes, and trauma, and the reflection in the mirror changes drastically.

However, despite the issues we face we do need to take care of our bodies. Because we are born again, they are the dwellings, or as the Bible calls them, the temples of the Holy Spirit. And it's best to care for yourself for the purpose serving the Lord. It's about being a testimony to the abundant life in Christ and using your body, your temple, as the illustration. Your body gives you the platform from which to speak, to work, and to pray. It is your temporary tent until you get your new body in heaven, if you are born again in this life.

You need to take care of your body. If we do not take care of our bodies and ourselves we won't have the energy to serve God and others. It's difficult to be useful bound to the sofa, the sick bed, or the computer screen, when it is in our power to get up and do the work we should do.

How should one take care of the body? No secret or magic formula will lead to success on how to do this. And, to save you a lot of expense and disappointment, realize that no magic pill or food can give you "amazing overnight results" as some of the ads for pills and potions claim. The key is what doctors and health professionals tell us: eat well, get enough rest, exercise, and reduce stress. That's it. It is so simple, yet so difficult to do. The daily decisions we make are far more powerful in our lives than an occasional big decision we make once in awhile. So make a daily decision to be healthy and to take care of yourself.

What I am saying has nothing to do with the quest for a perfect body, or the frenzied pursuit of achieving what our society defines as beauty. I am talking about the health and care of your body, which begins with caring for your soul and spirit. If you are healthy and spiritually and mentally whole on the inside, this will reflect on the outside, regardless of body type or shape.

Much distortion is on this subject in our sex-saturated culture that idolizes youthfulness; it's hard for me to even address this subject amidst the shouting messages you've already heard. And it's hard for you to hear me, precious daughter, because I am trying to talk through your preconceived ideas and the imprinting your brain has already received in our fallen, twisted world regarding your body. I wish we could wash away the wrong beliefs and distortions of how we think about our bodies and their functions, and learn from a clean, pure slate regarding what the Bible says we are and how we are to view our bodies. In Christ, we can be pure and holy because Jesus has washed us and made us clean. We are treasured in God's sight regardless of the body we have been given and are valued and of infinite worth to Him.

It's important to know you are already beautiful. Each young woman holds her own intrinsic beauty. You are beautiful and complete because you are made in God's image. He loves, treasures, and values you.

Many overemphasize the care and appearance of their bodies, and many have used them as instruments to sin. Instead of practicing self-control, we have lost our way while giving little attention to the real thing that matters the most and lasts forever— our spirits and souls. The Fall so succinctly described in Genesis of how we were forced out of the garden of Eden has taken us so far from how it is supposed to be. When we each take care of our spirit, manage our emotions, and allow God to love and redeem us, this healing and love will manifest itself in our physical bodies.

Until you reach the gates of pearl, take care of yourself, and use your body to serve God and others. *And* give yourself permission to make the time to take care of yourself. No one wants to be around a tired, worn out, frayed and frazzled, grouchy woman. I don't even want to be around myself when I'm like this.

You were made in God's image. You are adequate. You are enough. Be content with how you look. Do not be deceived and fall into the enemy's trap of believing the body is all there is. We are body, soul, and spirit. The body is temporary. Your spirit lasts forever. When Jesus told Nicodemus that he must be born again to see the kingdom of God and have eternal life, he was talking about his spirit, not his body (see John 3:3-8).

I strongly suggest that you guard your heart and your body. Honor it and care for it like God wants you to. Feed it healthy food, and give it rest. Listen to your body when it says it is hungry, tired, or needs to go to the bathroom. Take the time to care for yourself, even when it's not convenient. Figure out the unique pace you can maintain, and don't compare yourself to others who have more energy than you've got. We all get tired. We all reach our limits eventually. Give yourself permission to take care of yourself spiritually, mentally, emotionally, and physically.

What is true beauty? A woman who loves the Lord and has a kind spirit is truly beautiful. You are my precious daughter, regardless of how you look. You are valuable. You are enough.

"For the Lord sees not as man sees: man looks on the outward appearance, but the Lord looks on the heart" (1 Samuel 16:7).

"Or do you not know that your body is a temple of the Holy Spirit within you, whom you have from God? You are not your own, for you were bought with a price. So glorify God in your body" (1 Corinthians 6:19-20).

"Do not offer the parts of your body to sin, as instruments of wickedness, but rather offer yourselves to God, as those who have been brought from death to life; and offer the parts of your body to him as instruments of righteousness" (Romans 6:13 NIV).

Jesus said: "Come to me, all who labor and are heavy laden, and I will give you rest. Take my yoke upon you, and learn from me, for I am gentle and lowly in heart, and you will find rest for your souls. For my yoke is easy, and my burden is light" (Matthew 11:28-30).

5

Modesty in an Immodest World

I am about to tell you what I wish someone would have told me when I was young. I did not appreciate the value of modesty until I was beyond college. I know most of what I am about to say will sound outdated, impossible, and overreaching as far as modesty goes, but it *is not*. We've already discussed this subject, and as a mother it's a big part of raising a daughter. I want the best for you, and modesty plays a big role in who we are as women and how others perceive us. We can honor or dishonor ourselves, others, and God by how we speak, act and dress, and much of modesty is portrayed by clothing choices.

Modesty starts on the inside. It is realizing our intrinsic value because we are made in God's image, and for no other reason. We human beings are valuable, precious, and loved because He made us, not because of our looks, talents, skills, or physical attributes—or lack of them.

Your dad and I have spent a lot of time developing character in you and your brothers and very little time on praising your looks or drawing attention to your physical appearances. I did not comment on your looks or physical features until it was time to talk about it, and you asked me. Trying to preserve the innocence of childhood for as long as possible I put off commenting on your looks or your clothing choices until I had to. I wanted the focus to be who you are on the inside, not how you appear on the outside.

Here are some practical things we did to teach you modesty that you probably didn't notice.

- We focused on character development and enjoying childhood when you were young.

- We were careful about idolizing brand names over non-brand name clothing that basically serves the same purpose and is cheaper—which comes in handy now that you are a teenager. This obsession with only wearing name brands draws attention to image and not to character.

- From the time you were in kindergarten, we taught you to stay dressed as you walked around the house and to shut your door when you were changing your clothes. You have brothers, and they often had their friends over.

- If your door was shut, we honored your privacy by knocking first before we opened the door. This taught you to respect privacy: yours and others'.

- We taught you to wear appropriate clothing for whatever you were doing or where you were going.

- We limited your screen time so you were not feasting on the media's airbrushed images of what the world thinks a female body should look like. Such looks are not possible without airbrushing images and photo editing. Monitoring the small screen was a must. We realized that it is a monster that will devour you; it would eat you alive with the pressure of comparisons and kill your brain with porn. Too much pressure and porn are out there if we allowed you unlimited time on social media.

- We taught you table manners, phone etiquette, how to make proper introductions, as well as kindness, generosity, helpfulness, and thankfulness towards God and others. These are also part of modesty.

Modesty involves how we speak, how we dress, how we carry ourselves, and how we act. It's more than clothing choices; it's a lifestyle. It's your overall presentation to the world. In many areas, it's bringing it down a notch, withholding a bit, erring on the side of just a bit less. It's pausing before we speak, take action, or decide what to wear that day and thinking about each of these things before we hurriedly do them.

Clothing plays a big part of modesty, because that is one of the first things people notice about us. What is modest? What should you wear or not wear? Modest clothing doesn't mean oversized, colorless, and out of style. It just means modest. It's possible to wear clothes that compliment the body and look good without sacrificing modesty.

Revealing more skin does not increase our self-worth. Showing less skin increases the respect we receive from others; showing too much skin will reduce or eliminate respect. This is not how we think it should be or what we want. This is just a fact about how the world works.

Modesty is not only how we dress, but it involves character, speech, and decisions made about how we present ourselves in each area of our lives. Modesty gives us freedom to be ourselves and allows others to get to know us from the inside out. We feel better when others respect and and value us, and that's what modesty does for us. It helps us value our bodies and ourselves. It gives us approachability in the presence of others. It puts focus on who we are on the inside, not how we look on the outside. It calms our outer presence so our inner self can shine through.

I know that at times finding clothing that is modest is difficult. While you and I have been shopping, it has been hard to find modest clothing that is stylish and looks good in the teen section of the clothing stores. We have discussed that low-cut, tight T-shirts, short shorts, bra straps that show, miniskirts, and crop tops are not modest.

I am thankful that we can talk about modesty and that you eventually listen when I gently tell you that you should think twice about what you are wearing. I realize that you may not appreciate the benefit of modesty until you are an adult or when you are raising a daughter of your own.

Setting guidelines and rules regarding modesty is not giving you a list of rules that you will be forced to keep, but it's akin to giving you the rules of the road so you will avoid accidents and harm while driving a car. Modesty protects you and the young men around you.

Our choices in how we dress reflect our internal values. If you show others and the guys around you through how your dress that you respect yourself, most likely they will show you respect. When we practice modesty, we are asking others around us to treat us with respect and it shows that we want them to know who we are on the inside.

I resolved while you were young that I am your mother first, then your friend second. I hope that when you reach adulthood and are out of the nest we will have a smooth transition from the mother/daughter relationship to a peer-to-peer friendship. I am teaching you about the often difficult subject of modesty because I love you and want what's best for you. I have been watching out for you.

And don't worry, I am also working with you to grow and develop your femininity and beauty. Your dad threatened to dress you in burlap, wool socks, and Army boots and to leave your teeth crooked and your hair in a snarl. When boys started noticing you, he would fret and stew about it. First, because he couldn't get over the fact that his little girl was growing up, and second, because only a man realizes what a testosterone-loaded teenage boy is thinking. No matter what others say about how you conduct yourself or what clothes you wear, modesty matters.

This effort of teaching you character development and modesty will give you some of the guidance and safety you need to navigate the treacherous waters of childhood, adolescence, and the teenage years. This will hopefully help you arrive at adulthood whole and intact spiritually, mentally, emotionally, and physically.

I know we will get through this and be the best of friends very soon, and you will realize the benefits of modesty. As a mother, it can be an uphill battle, but I know this will be worthwhile, and you will be blessed as your life is lived before others in the attitude of modesty.

"And why are you anxious about clothing?... Therefore do not be anxious, saying, 'What shall we eat?' or 'What shall we drink?' or 'What shall we wear?' For the Gentiles seek after all these things, and your heavenly Father knows that you need them all. But seek first the kingdom of God and his righteousness, and all these things will be added to you" (Matthew 6:28, 31-33).

6

It's Not about the Money

Money, money, money. In our culture, the dream would be to swim in it, or to have so much of it we'd wallpaper our houses with it just to boast that we have it. In our nation, we build houses that are almost castles, buy cars that kings could ride in, and wear the finest clothes— for the love of money. Lottery advertisements shout at us, trying to capture our attentions and promising that if we had truckloads of money, our problems would evaporate, and oh so happy we would be.

Money's lure can be so sweet; but its results are deceptive. In America, success is measured in dollars, and those who have reached the list of richest people in the nation are seen as the truly successful. Everyone else is viewed as lesser on the scale, lower in rank, smaller in worth.

In the world's eyes, important people have lots of money. Unimportant people have little money. We measure successes, failures, achievements, and happiness in dollars. We seek to fill voids, longing for riches to satisfy our insatiable appetites for money. Oh, how far we have wandered.

Money will lose its value in heaven. In America, our currency is technically backed by gold. In heaven, the streets are paved with it. Gold is nothing but asphalt and concrete there.

Statistics say that most lottery winners are bankrupt in five years. They are not happier, and have strained family and friend relationships. This love of money has divided households, churches, cities, and nations.

Yes, in America people strive for elegant houses and nice things. They enjoy talking about the latest trendy fashions and strive to wear beautiful clothes made from wool, silk, and cotton. People strive for the latest electronic gadgets, the best seats in stadiums, and the most recent sports car. Yes, our country has a bounty of delicious food. But it's not about the money.

Money has a lure like no other. People will make fools of themselves, enter enticing contests where they have microscopic chances of winning, and divorce spouses over the pursuit of money. Some will do daily stock trading via the internet in hopes to make fast money. Our culture seems saturated with those who want to make fast money and a lot of it, but this rarely works or produces the happiness people are seeking. As sand through the hourglass of time, so money passes through the hands of fools.

The only way to get money honestly and successfully is to earn it. Work and obedience produce money and reward, not entering the lottery, gambling, or trying to gain a fast buck by bypassing the system of finding good jobs and earning money.

Once you have earned money, it is necessary to learn the fine art of tithing it, saving it, investing it, spending it, and giving it away. That's the only way to successfully manage and keep what you have earned to make it grow and multiply.

After many years of painful mistakes and racking up credit card debt, your dad and I have learned the art of handling money. We struggled, lost or quit jobs, and made some bad financial decisions. Later, after taking some classes and applying sound financial principles to our money, we learned to manage it. Subsequently, years later and handling money as God instructs, we are now debt free. Our home mortgage is paid off, our cars are paid for, we have no credit card debt, and we give regularly to church and charities every month. This was not an accomplishment that came because we won the lottery or because we tried schemes to get a fast buck, but from daily discipline over a long period of time.

What I have discovered about money is that it is a *tool* to buy material possessions we need and to spread the gospel, just as hammers and nails and saws are tools to build houses and buildings. Money cannot satisfy our longing for happiness and fulfillment. Only the Lord can lastingly fill the vacuum in our souls for contentment and peace, and only God can remove the fear of not having enough. Watch others try to fill this longing with money, and you will soon see it doesn't work.

What I value in life cannot be measured in dollars or gained with having more money. What I value is the Lord Jesus Christ, your wonderful dad, all our kids, and the awesome family and friends the Lord has given us. Beyond this, nothing will last, especially if you can buy it with money.

We have many Scriptures to choose from, and Jesus had so much to say about money and possessions. Here are a few verses:

"No one can serve two masters, for either he will hate the one and love the other, or he will be devoted to the one and despise the other. You cannot serve God and money" (Matthew 6:24).

"For the love of money is a root of all kinds of evils. It is through this craving that some have wandered away from the faith and pierced themselves with many pangs" (1 Timothy 6:10).

"He who loves money will not be satisfied with money,

nor he who loves wealth with his income;

This also is vanity" (Ecclesiastes 5:10).

"And the twelve gates were twelve pearls, each of the gates made of a single pearl, and the street of the city was pure gold, transparent as glass" (Revelation 21:21).

"As for the rich in this present age, charge them not to be haughty, nor to set their hopes on the uncertainty of riches, but on God, who richly provides us with everything to enjoy. They are to do good, to be rich in good works, to be generous and ready to share, thus storing up treasure for themselves as a good foundation for the future, so that they may take hold of that which is truly life" (1 Timothy 6:17-19).

7

Time and the Sabbath Rest

When you reach adulthood and have attempted to manage your life and the life of your family, someone somewhere along the way will eventually say, "Time is money". Loads of books, websites, and seminars are available on how to earn, manage, save, and invest money. Also lots of books, both secular and Christian, are available on how to manage time. Notice that time is different than money. Time can be managed, not earned, saved, or invested for later. But with God it can be!

When one of your brothers was a baby, your dad and I took a two-day class on money management. From this class and author Larry Burkett's books on money management, we decided to work ourselves out of debt, including credit card debt so we could be better stewards of the money we had. We also wanted more money to do the things and have the things we wanted. We thought more money would solve our debt problems.

The key, the foundation, the absolute starting point was to give the first 10 percent of our earnings to the Lord, called the *tithe*. Naturally, this did not make sense, to give money away while we were in debt. But following the commands outlined and explained in Scripture, we gave God the first ten percent of our earnings. When we did this and gave up clutching it to ourselves, we began to learn His ways of handling money.

We did this at church, our second home, and everything changed. Your dad and I agreed on a budgeting plan and stuck to it. But what surprised us the most was that while we were working our way out of debt, we had enough money each month. It was amazing, and I cannot explain in the natural how it worked out. The math just did not add up. The bank statement said we would be short, but we weren't. Even our clothes did not wear out until the very month we were out of credit card debt. We were still paying off the mortgage, but at least we had every other area under control.

One thing we learned is that having more money was not going to solve our money problems. More money would just make our poor money management skills have worse consequences. More money wasn't the answer, but handling the money we currently had efficiently and effectively according to

God's plan was the answer. By tithing, handling, investing and saving our money as God outlines in Scripture, we have now enjoyed over fifteen years of being debt free. It feels so good.

What does this have to do with the Sabbath rest? For years I was exhausted, overcommitted and frustrated. I needed more time to get everything done that I thought needed to be done. You three kids were little, and I was on the run every day, all day. The motherhood fatigue of having three small kids at home was overwhelming.

When you were about three years old, I experienced a series of events and teachings about the sovereignty of God and the infallibility of Scripture. Among many other things, I decided to begin honoring the Sabbath day, one of the Ten Commandments. I knew and respected the other nine and realized they were still very important, but God gave us ten. I thought that honoring the Sabbath was not something that God would change His mind about. After all, He wrote the commandments with His finger on stone tablets and gave them to Moses, and in that day anyone that profaned the Sabbath was put to death. Surely, something written by God in stone was important, and the Sabbath was declared a day of solemn rest holy to the Lord.

How could I honor the Sabbath as a non-Jewish woman in the twenty-first century living in America? No one around me even used the word sabbath let alone try and honor it. What could I do to honor God in this area? Was this even important in our highly automated culture? After all, we no longer are plowing the fields by hand or growing our own cotton to make our own clothing.

When I was a girl, most stores and gas stations were closed on Sundays. Some of the leftover respect for the Blue Laws were in place that had been repealed in 1966 in our state. Many could not imagine going shopping, and no sporting events were scheduled for Sunday. Many just assumed much of life was going to come to a grinding halt one day per week, and few were expected to work unless it was for the hospital, police, or fire department. Communities paused for Sunday, and not many people were out and about.

After realizing that the Sabbath day must still be a big deal to God, since it was one of the Ten Commandments, I thought I would try and honor it. So I would not do what I considered work on Sundays. I did not grocery shop, do laundry, wash dishes, cook a meal, go to work, use the computer, vacuum, pay bills, or clean house. I would not go into stores to do heavy shopping and engage in commerce that could wait for another day, nor would I plan the work I needed to do the rest of the week. I would give my body and brain a break from the stresses of work and focus on God, family, and people.

I quickly realized that if I wanted to rest on Sundays, I had to organize the other six days of the week! I could not use Sundays to catch up on the other work I had put off or neglected. I started doing much more planning and work to make better use of the time the other six days of the week— watch less TV, get up earlier, plan ahead for dinners, discipline myself to keep the house and kitchen clean at least once a day, and teach the boys how to help me. You also started to learn to work at small chores when you were about four or five years old.

At first you kids complained because suddenly Sundays were slower and "boring". We no longer were dashing to the next needless distracting destination or to the store to get a snack because the rest of the food in the house was not interesting enough. I wanted to honor God by honoring the Sabbath, and these other activities and work could wait. As you got older, you would beg me to go shopping so we could have "mother/daughter" time, and you thought pulling on my mama heart strings would get me to change my mind, but I held fast and said no.

After I started recognizing and honoring the Sabbath, many things improved. The week now had a rhythm, and the days and weeks didn't run together so much. Time was more paced, and I got more done realizing I had to work for the six days I was given so I *could* rest on the seventh! By honoring the Sabbath, it forced me to get all else done during the other six days of the week and not be lazy. No longer could Sunday be a catch-up day for the neglected work, laundry, and cleaning that didn't get done during the week.

Over time I also noticed that your dad and you kids took a Sabbath, too, because as you saw me sitting or napping, it slowed your pace down. It's wonderful to slow the pace, have long talks with each other, play games, and enjoy the Lord and His blessings together, especially the blessing of rest.

And it all got done. How? The clock never said I would have enough time to accomplish it all. It is very hard to explain in the natural how there was enough money to go around while we were deep in debt and began to tithe. It is also very hard to explain in the natural how there was enough time to get the work done.

The Lord has multiplied my time when I have asked Him so I could get it all done. He has also cut the time short when I have needed to move on, and He has made time pass quickly when I had a very long drive in the car by myself—especially after a long, grueling day at work. He has almost stopped time too, when I have wanted just a few more minutes with your dad before he's had to leave for the week to work. There weren't a few more minutes, but God made them in the supernatural.

Financially, money is easy to chart, put in neat columns on paper, count, and keep track of via online banking. But time is so hard to keep track of, to chart, to capture. It escapes even when we are paying attention. Time keeps passing even when we don't want it to. It is our job to capture the time we are given, to make something useful, and to be a blessing to others with the time we are given.

God is in control of time and of all of our days. He even lengthened one day for Joshua. Joshua needed more time and asked God for it. Joshua "said in the sight of Israel, 'Sun, stand still at Gibeon, and moon, in the Valley of Aijalon.' And the sun stood still, and the moon stopped, until the nation took vengeance on their enemies. Is this not written in the Book of Jashar? The sun stopped in the midst of heaven and did not hurry to set for about a whole day. There has been no day like it before or since, when the Lord heeded the voice of a man, for the Lord fought for Israel" (Joshua 10:12-14).

God has charted our days for us and decided the time and place we were to be born. "For you formed my inward parts; you knitted me together in my mother's womb" (Psalm 139:13). This verse tells me that He planned you and me, all of us. He knows us and also knows we are living a life encased in time. We cannot escape it, live outside of it, or control it.

By honoring the Sabbath day, we can fulfill His purposes for us, capture the time, and invest it for Him. Time is a free gift from God, this gift of a day.

Remember the Sabbath day and keep it for the Lord, and He will give you rest. How will you observe the Sabbath day so you can honor God in this way? He is the God of time.

"That he might make you know that man does not live by bread alone, but man lives by every word that comes from the mouth of the Lord. Your clothing did not wear out on you and your foot did not swell these forty years. So you shall keep the commandments of the Lord your God by walking in his ways and by fearing him" (Deuteronomy 8:3-4,6).

8

Struggles in the Dark

his will happen. Guaranteed. You will have times when it's very dark, when it's hard to find hope, when there is no encouragement to be found or heard. It's that time of life when it is hard to go on. The walls of your mind shut you in, and hopelessness is your breakfast, lunch, and dinner. This can be due to a mistake of your own making or through no fault of your own. It just is.

There is no way to avoid it. It is part of the human condition. I have struggled with darkness and depression of the soul off and on my whole life. Reading the psalms, I realize that this has been a problem for people for thousands of years. Remembering this can be a comfort.

How do we climb out of darkness? Make it flee? Many solutions have been tried through the ages, yet the struggle with the dark remains.

The answer is what the Scriptures tell us. We need to look up to the Lord. This may seem like an unusual answer to the problems we humans face, and you can try a lot of other solutions that appear to be better. But only one person has ever successfully overcome darkness, and His name is Jesus.

We need a Savior from this darkness and from our fallen human conditions. He is the only one with the power and authority to overcome darkness. The world offers a million other answers, but allow me to save you a lot of wasted time and tell you He is the only lasting, effective, permanent, always-available answer to this.

What has caused the darkness in the first place? Sometimes it helps to start there. Maybe you need to repent of sin and get rid of your guilt. Are you feeling guilty because you have sinned? Or are you fighting the enemy, who is the king of darkness? Sometimes these two are hard to discern.

The next thing to do is to call a friend. Overcome the sluggishness that accompanies darkness by making contact with a trusted friend. Your dad and I are this help when you are young. Then later, you can add godly girlfriends who are mature women into your circle of friends. When you marry, add your husband to those who love you. God will keep adding people to your life if you let Him.

I also found that I have received a lot of light and attained understanding through books. An author somewhere has expressed much of what we struggle with. Sometimes the only friend I had was a good book, because people can get too busy or are unable or unwilling, and have little time for others who need them. I thank God especially for the godly people who have written books about their lives, their own struggles, and their own walks of faith.

What a blessing to read about others who have gone before us and endured the struggles to reach the other side and come out better for it. I am so thankful for those who took the time to write these down and preserve them for us sojourners who would come after them. So much understanding, relief, joy ,and life has come to me because I have read so many fabulous books. Get some great books!

What I also do when I am in the dark is I start praising the Lord. I sing the worship songs I know, and read Scripture out loud. This doesn't change the circumstance that I am in, but it does change my perspective. God helps me to see a bigger picture rather than my own narrow view of the circumstances. I often wonder if praise and worship improve my brain chemistry and the chemical balance in my body. It can be that much of a change for me.

I find that screen time often makes this worse. Screen time, social media, or watching movies in an attempt to escape often doesn't work. People who love and care about you are the cure for helping to chase away darkness and loneliness, not screen time.

Another step that can help overcome this darkness of soul is to do something kind or thoughtful for someone else. "Whoever brings blessing will be enriched, and one who waters will himself be watered" (Proverbs 11:25). So if you need to be enriched and watered in your soul, do it for someone else.

Another thing that helps is mixing all of the above with time. Passing time is a blessing when mixed with Jesus, those who love you, and praise and worship. Sometimes time passed in distraction in something uplifting can also help dispel the darkness.

I hate depression and lack of hope. I absolutely hate it. I abhor it with every cell in my body. I don't mean dark as at night but that dark feeling in your soul that can drain life away in a matter of minutes and take away desire to go on. The darkness in my soul often threatens to rear its ugly head and swallow my future and me. It has been a struggle much of my life.

That's why I love Jesus so much because He is the exact opposite of this. He is nothing but light. Revelation says that heaven has no need of sun or moon because He is our light.

How permeating. How wonderful. And His light penetrates our souls to the cores of the places no one can see. It is wonderful, Claire. Hopefully by the time you read this, you will have experienced His light in your soul regularly. I hope dark times for you are few. But if you do find yourself in the dark, remember if you choose to do something about it, most likely that dark place will be temporary.

Walking in the light has little to do with our outward circumstances, our appearance, or what is going on in the world. It is an inner decision to follow Jesus regardless of what is happening to us or the circumstances we are in. It is being an overcomer in the midst of struggles and having faith while living in a faithless world. It is deciding to follow Jesus regardless of how you feel. It is living for Him, the God of light.

"The eye is the lamp of the body. So, if your eye is healthy, your whole body will be full of light, but if your eye is bad, your whole body will be full of darkness. If then the light in you is darkness, how great is the darkness!" (Matthew 6:22-23).

"For at one time you were darkness, but now you are light in the Lord. Walk as children of light" (Ephesians 5:8).

"If I say, 'Surely the darkness will cover me, and the light about me be night,' even the darkness is not dark to you; the night is bright as the day, for darkness is as light with you" (Psalm 139:11-12).

"And the city has no need of sun or moon to shine on it, for the glory of God gives it light, and its lamp is the Lamb. By its light will the nations walk, and the kings of the earth will bring their glory into it, and its gates will never be shut by day—and there will be no night there" (Revelation 21:23-25).

9

Friendships

Friendships with women are wonderful, warming, comforting, and needed for our spiritual, mental, and emotional health. Friendship is a skill that takes many years to develop. Many of us have suffered from the mean and ugly things done to us from other girls and women who we thought were our friends, or family members who had our undeserved trust. I encourage you to separate yourself from the mean ones, find healing and push past the hurt, and pursue uplifting and encouraging friends. We need friends.

We women are the keeper of friendships, the barometers of relationships. We seek out friendships among women much more than men seek friendships with other men. A long talk with great girlfriends can fuel us for a week. These conversations refresh our souls and give us the relational oxygen we long for.

If we haven't seen good friends for a while, when we do finally see them we are filled with joy, so excited to finally be with them in person. Being reunited with good friends is so warming and pleasant.

We like sitting at little tea tables and talking for hours with our women friends. If a few of us are invited to a sporting event, usually with the guys, we spend a lot of time in the stands talking with our women friends, with only one eye on the game. Why would we sit for hours watching a sporting event and not take advantage of that time to talk to our women friends? This is a no brainer for us, while I've heard the men amongst us comment, "That was sure an expensive ticket we bought so you could sit and talk with your friends!"

Watching parting scenes at airports, rare is the man in tears who is saying good-bye to a loved one or a good friend. More often the woman is in tears, openly expressing herself. We are usually not inhibited expressing how we feel about those we love, especially when we are parting.

Reaching out to find women friends is worth the vulnerability and risk. Going to a new school, starting a new job, or moving to a new town puts us in a weak place. But remember, extending yourself and reaching out to other women to find friends is worth it.

As relationships are built over time, we come to the understanding of what real friends are. Real friends are steady, faithful, honest, trustworthy, do not gossip, and permanent. Let's look at these more closely:

- *Steady.* These reliable friends can be counted on through thick and thin and through changing seasons. They like you for you, not for what you can do for them or what they can get from you. They have pure motives, and they don't change their minds about friendship with you during small disagreements. They are not only consistent in their beliefs and motives, but also they are consistent in how they treat you.

- *Faithful.* These types of friends will back you and want what is best for you, even if you aren't sure what that is for yourself at times. They will not abandon you for guys or shove you aside when other, more appealing or exciting friends come along. They will keep their word, and if they make plans with you, they won't ditch you if someone or something more exciting comes along, without a good and credible explanation for doing so.

- *Honest.* These friends are truth tellers and will tell the truth even if it costs them some stress or embarrassment. They strive to be honest and are not pretending to like

49

you because they want something from you or want to get to know your cute brother. They don't lie to you or bait you to do something you don't want to do.

- *Trustworthy.* You can trust these friends. Trust is built over time, shared experiences, and working towards a common goal together. Without trust, there is no friendship. Friendships can endure stress, differences of opinion, or space caused by time or distance, but they cannot endure without trust.

- *Void of Gossip.* I have watched friendships crash because of gossip. It is a fire that burns and scorches everyone involved — people who are objects of the gossip, the persons who tell the gossip, and the hearers. It is a friendship killer, and I suggest avoiding gossip with everything in your power to do so. Do not start it, repeat it, and change the subject or leave the conversation if someone is spreading it. It is this deadly. Women who gossip inherently cannot be trusted. If they are willing to tell confidences about others while you listen, what are they saying about you when you are not around? Gossip is deadly to relationships. Avoid it.

Temporary friends are unpredictable and non-permanent. They may be dishonest, and can't keep confidences. They soon fade out of your life, because it's difficult to develop friendships where there is no trust and when trust continues to be undermined or broken. Throwing friendships off balance, it's just too much work to maintain friendships with these types of women, and eventually they end. Also, it's okay to walk away from these women. Don't feel guilty for reducing the drama you are exposed to and taking steps to maintain your sanity.

Many girls and women who have been hurt in the past by other women, and sometimes their own mothers, often have trouble developing or maintaining friendships with women. Their relational wounds and scars are too painful to run the risk of opening up again to other women. You will notice them as you reach adulthood and meet lots of different kinds of women. If you meet a cold or distant woman, just remember that something in her past has caused her to be this way, and go easy on her. Extend lots of grace and gentleness to her, and treat her with kindness. She needs the friendships of other women, but she just doesn't know how to go about it.

Emotionally whole and relationally healthy women I know have close, reliable women friends. Those women who are struggling and having mental and/or emotional problems usually are isolated and do not have close women friends. Friendships often help us keep our sanity and may reduce our need for counseling or professional help when we are struggling.

Friendships with women have warmed me and comforted me through many years. Often, we are closer to our women friends than to members of our own families. This is because we get to choose our friends and find those like-minded girls and women to share our lives with. Don't feel guilty about this. Every person in your life will be different from the next, and each will fill a different role in your life.

I haven't begun to tell you how to repair a broken friendship or how to manage and grow a good friendship. But I think you get my point that we women love our friendships with other women when they are life-giving and a blessing to our lives. Highly value friendship, and don't easily give up on good friends. They are worth more than gold.

"Greater love has no one than this, that someone lay down his life for his friends" (John 15:13).

"Faithful are the wounds of a friend; profuse are the kisses of an enemy…Do not forsake your friend and your father's friend" (Proverbs 27:6,10).

"Therefore encourage one another and build one another up, just as you are doing" (1 Thessalonians 5:11).

"A dishonest man spreads strife, and a whisperer separates close friends" (Proverbs 16:28).

10

Be Your Own Best Friend.

*W*ow. So many people now have heads down, eyes on little screens that they carry in their hands everywhere they go. They even trip and fall walking down sidewalks because they are busy looking at the little screens. Remember the student at your high school that was struck by a car while crossing a busy road outside of a crosswalk because she had her headphones in and was staring at her smart phone? Amazingly she was able to walk away from the accident!

Looking out over a crowd of people in public places, we notice that very few have their heads up to even see what is happening around them. At malls, bus stops, cafeterias, airports, sporting events, and during family meals at restaurants people are staring at their smart phones while the world passes them by. Ignoring those they are with, they silently stare at their screens while companionship and friendship are around them.

When I was young, I would get together with my girl-friends, and we would talk up a storm because we didn't have the instant communication ability that you have now. We had time between conversations and seeing one another to actually miss each other and really be happy to see each other once we did get together! And then when we were together, we *talked* uninterrupted. I'm actually feel sad for your generation, as you do so much texting and social media surfing that it fills the time you do have together. Cell phones are allowed to interrupt your time together, your conversation, and your train of thought. And I'm not even mentioning the misunderstandings and poor communication that happens because someone was misunderstood in a text. What's missing during texting is the tone of voice, eye contact, body language, expressions, and the other things we read and observe in one another to communicate when we are face to face.

This screen time does not satisfy the companionship and friendship needs we want and desire. Studies tell us we are lonelier when too much time is spent staring at screens. They provide false companionship.

I would encourage you to fight this more than ever, these hours upon hours of giving our lives to our screens, because I don't think we realize as a society what this is going to do to us over the long haul. So, what can you do?

One of the things I learned as a child and young adult was to be my own friend. That's what we did when we were bored as kids and teenagers when we didn't have lit screens to entertain and distract us and finding friends or willing siblings that day wasn't an option. We couldn't touch screens to quickly forget our boredom, loneliness, or friendlessness. We had to make our own entertainment. Over time, what develops is what I call being one's own best friend.

What do I mean by this? The Bible says to love your neighbor as yourself. So that signals to me that we need to love ourselves. We need to have worked through our hurts and guilt enough and to develop skills so that being by ourselves is not an exercise in torture. Being alone for short periods of time is something that we can come to like and be okay with when it presents itself without running to screens as knee-jerk reactions to fill the boredom or loneliness we are feeling at the moment. We humans love stimulation, but constant stimulation is not good. The hand-held phone has been a catalyst to play into this unchecked weakness.

How can we love ourselves if we have never spent any time with ourselves? How can you truly love someone else unless you have received that love, companionship, and friendship from the Lord that's needed for healthy relationships?

It is wise to spend time fostering a friendship with yourself, so to speak, and treat yourself this way and in so doing, to enrich yourself. What you are doing is quieting your heart and allowing God to be found in the stillness. The psalmist David ministered to himself as shown in this verse: "But David strengthened himself in the Lord his God" (1 Samuel 30:6). We would benefit from doing this also. He was a friend to himself when finding friends was difficult.

I enjoy spending time by myself, doing what interests me at home for short periods of time. But please don't misunderstand and think that this was always enjoyable. I learned contentment in the midst of difficult situations. Friends are not only vital to mental health and growth, but also are blessings and gifts from God. Take care to build up and nurture your friendships, but it is also a benefit to take the time to develop disciplines and constructive hobbies for yourself when the option for companionship or friendship is not available.

Can't be your own best friend because guilt, remorse, depression, anxiety, or life's circumstances have given you a blow to the gut, derailed your train, or crashed in on your house? Or maybe you have not taken the time to reflect and get away from the screen to even know how you are feeling or what your deeper thoughts are. That's the best time to be a friend to yourself and take care of what is bothering or hurting you. Pray and pour your heart out to God, call a friend, ask God for the wisdom you need, see a good counselor, join a prayer group, or call me! But work it out, work past the resistance, and pursue God in the solitude, while avoiding the screen. Lean on others. Talk to people face-to-face. These actions are some ways to be a good friend to yourself.

We may find it difficult to slow down and quiet ourselves so we can even take inventory of where our hearts and minds have been dwelling. In these times, remember to extend the same grace and mercy to yourself that you would give your good friend. We women are so hard on ourselves and often carry the backpack of guilt. I constantly fight it too. But we need to dump the load of guilt and condemnation at the foot of the cross, take up Jesus's cross, and follow Him. Otherwise we will get stuck under the load of life and not fulfill what He has for us, let alone anyone else.

You are a lovely, patient, kind, warm, and generous friend to many already. Don't forget to be that to yourself, especially when you are hungry, angry, lonely, or tired. If you are one or more of these four things, do something about it, and take care of yourself before you move onto other things. Give yourself permission to love yourself, be a friend to yourself, and for our sakes, take care of yourself.

Be the friend to others that you would like to have, and treat yourself in light of who God says you are.

"Be still, and know that I am God" (Psalm 46:10).

"Then Jesus told his disciples, 'If anyone would come after me, let him deny himself and take up his cross and follow me. For whoever would save his life will lose it, but whoever loses his life for my sake will find it' " (Matthew 16:24-25).

"And Jesus said, "You shall not murder, You shall not commit adultery, You shall not steal, You shall not bear false witness, Honor your father and mother, and, You shall love your neighbor as yourself' " (Matthew 19:18-19).

"Love is patient and kind; love does not envy or boast, it is not arrogant or rude. It does not insist on its own way; it is not irritable or resentful; it does not rejoice at wrongdoing, but rejoices with the truth. Love bears all things, believes all things, hopes all things, endures all things. Love never ends" (1 Corinthians 13:4-8).

11

Movies

"Let's watch a movie!" someone says, inviting you to a time of escape from your duties to find entertainment. Ah! What fun!

I estimate I have watched hundreds of movies in my life, some on the big screen in the theater, but most at home from the comfort of our own sofa. I'm not necessarily proud of the fact that I have watched so many movies. Some have been fabulous and well written and acted, and contain some of the most wonderful music written by human creativity. You and I have enjoyed hours watching the girl movies we now reminisce about together. I have watched some of them multiple times, but most movies weren't worth the time I gave them. I often think what I could have done with the time that would have been more constructive and impacting.

Movies are powerful conveyors of messages: good and evil. They have transformed our culture and the American landscape, affecting most of what we think and know. They have shaped our psyches more than we realize, as we are saturated in them. Movies can be wonderful or evil and destructive. Either way, they suck us in and don't let go. Why do we love the lit screen with its action, storytelling, music, and beautiful people? We are fascinated with the screen, the visual effects, and the talented acting.

But I want to turn the corner, call you away from its enticement, and alert you to a few things. Please be careful what you watch, what you allow your eyes to see. Many images are in my mind that I wish I could get rid of that have been put there because of movies I watched. These images and messages have shaped my attitudes and views about relationships, sex, and how our bodies "should" look. These attitudes are rarely biblical when portrayed in a movie.

When going to a mall or out in public, many different kinds of people are seen – old, young, short, tall, fat, thin, and many races and ethnic backgrounds. In the movies and on TV, rarely anyone is just average – or too short or too tall, or what the world calls unattractive. People in the movies are usually young, gorgeous, handsome, look well, walk well, speak well, and appear to have few shortcomings or frailties. The images we see on the silver screen are hand picked and heavily made up. Actors get to do a scene for the camera over and over again until it is just right with no mistakes, no misspoken words, and no blunders. *But this is not real life! It's the movies.* Remember this.

The people on the screen are *acting*. They are saying rehearsed lines, and they know what the actors they are acting with are going to say next. Actors are simply in front of the cameras to deliver their prewritten lines in a highly skilled, rehearsed fashion. This is done in front of cameras after lots of practice and training and in front of lots of other people who are involved in the camera, sound, and lighting crews. While witnessing a scene on the screen between two people, realize these people are not alone as the screen portrays. The room they are filming in is filled with the behind-the-scenes crew who are telling them what positions to be in, where to walk, how to stand, how to speak, with cameras rolling while others operate the lighting and manage the sound. They deliver their lines over and over again in multiple takes until it is to the director's standards. This does not resemble real life at all.

A TV series not long ago was about a family's life in politics and some of the issues the writers of the show assumed this political family dealt with, the stresses and challenges that the writers and producers of the show assumed political families live with. I never watched the show. I only heard about it (you know me, not a big TV fan), and then an acquaintance I know saw me one day in the bookstore. She rushed up to me and said she *loved* the show and was happy because by watching the show she realized and understood some of the issues we face. She said watching the show helped her understand our family.

I just about choked on my response, realizing she was serious when she said this. I quickly gathered my composure and tried to not let my disbelief show on my face, gave a polite smile, said some benign comments, and changed the subject. I felt pity for her. She had confused a TV show with reality and thought that our lives were like what was portrayed. Really? What some writer/director/producer has put on TV is not reality. It's a story made for TV, loosely based on reality at best.

Movies and TV do a good job of telling a story, but they do *not* convey reality. Movies are not reality; they are the movies. Many people I know have blurred the images of movies with the reality of life— and it's to their disadvantage to do so. They have mistaken the movies as reality or truth and do not understand that a movie is a story from someone's imagination. People spend so much time in front of a screen watching non reality, and it shapes their value system without them realizing it. We are so drawn to the screen, while having little aware-ness of what it is doing to our value systems, our thoughts, our worldviews, and our consciences. The frog is being slowly boiled to death in the proverbial warming pot.

Everyone who produces, writes, edits, and offers a TV show or movie is promoting a specific and intentional worldview. Please be a discerning moviegoer and be intentional about protecting your eyes and mind from the false reality and distorted worldview that they are often promoting. These false realities created on the screen do not help to sharpen and improve your conscience, but erode and distort it. Remember, a movie simply tells a story and doesn't portray reality.

"Whatever is true, whatever is honorable, whatever is just, whatever is pure, whatever is lovely, whatever is commendable, if there is any excellence, if there is anything worthy of praise, think about these things" (Philippians 4:8).

12

The Media Monster

When I was a teenager, I formed an addiction to TV. I would come home from junior high school, get a snack, and plop down in front of the TV for the next couple of hours to watch the popular afternoon talk show that featured celebrities, the odd, the unusual, and the edgy.

I didn't have any friends at this point in my awkward teenage years. Friendships were difficult, and I didn't know how to be a friend. It was more interesting and entertaining to sit in a chair and get lost in the fantasy world of another's odd or exciting life through the television set. Since I was bored and lonely, I didn't know how to entertain myself or make friends.

Fast-forward to the early 1990s. I was now married and frequently homebound by two active toddlers. I had given my life to Christ, but didn't realize that I now had to let Him transform many areas of my life. One was a full-blown addiction to TV. I also did not understand how it was affecting the good relationship I wanted with Jesus or my worldview.

Beginning to feel a bit guilty about watching so much TV, I would appease my guilt by vacuuming during commercials, and picking up toys and clutter with the TV volume up so loud I wouldn't miss a word.

About this time, I attended a time management and get-your-life-in-order women's gathering at church. One of the activities they had us do was to chart out on a timeline what exactly we did with the hours in an average day. So I went home and did this. Boy, was I shocked! Without realizing it, I was watching TV at least four hours a day. I cheated on the chart and didn't write down all of the hours I actually did watch TV because I felt so guilty.

I knew I had a problem. I didn't know what to do about it, and I justified it in my mind and said to myself it wasn't really that bad. I wasn't hurting anyone, right? And besides, since I was bored and lonely, what was the harm in giving myself the treat of watching a little TV? It was just entertainment, anyway. And all the while I didn't realize that the monster of screen addiction had moved into my heart.

Then you were born. I was now attending the wonderful organization of Mothers of Preschoolers (MOPS), had made friends with lots of other moms who had kids at home, and wanted to live for Christ in everything. God had healed me of a lot of shame and pain from my childhood, and my life was benefitting from the transformational power of Christ. It was more evident than ever that I had to give up the TV. But, I had full-blown arguments in my head over it.

On top of the hours given to my responsibilities and TV watching was a dense fog of fatigue that plagued me every day. I was stressed and exhausted because I didn't have enough hours to do everything. The laundry, grocery shopping, cooking, cleaning, and caring for three busy kids was a lot of work, and I fell into bed every night exhausted.

I didn't realize how much I needed the three or four hours a day I was losing to TV to do other things. My TV addiction was in the jumbled mix of a busy home with three kids. I knew a problem was in there somewhere, but in the noise and busyness of my life I did not bring it out into the light to dealt with it.

Realizing I had to break this addiction, the only way I knew to disengage was to quit TV cold turkey. No screen time at all. So I did.

Half way through the next day, I was in shock. The withdrawals to my addiction were horrid. I was intensely lonely and felt like I had given up a friendship— a few friendships. It was painful, and I was mad that I had decided to give it up.

The mental torture was awful. And the pain of the withdrawals frightened me, because it showed me just how addicted I was. Just about then I discovered that *Focus on the Family* with Dr. James Dobson came on the radio at 9:00 a.m. each morning, so I began to listen to that to replace the false relationships I was missing by not watching TV. This radio show was my dose of truth for my heart and mind each day. And I learned so much. I replaced the TV watching time with listening to something that enriched my soul and helped to fill the lack of close relationships in my life.

Slowly, over time, I began to have better days without the TV. I realized that I was learning a lot of truth, once I put the noise and distraction of TV aside. I read my Bible more. I prayed more. I better organized the house and took the time to plan ahead for meals. I had more time for friends.

And I continued to listen to the radio. Dr. Dobson and his wise radio guests taught me so many things about God, marriage, child rearing, the home, relationships, friendships among women, and other things I hungered for. His radio show met a need I had but I didn't have the maturity to put this need into words. I knew I was missing so much in my heart and life. Remember, this is before hand-held phones, computers, iPads, the internet, social media, and hand-held electronic devices. The few ways to get information about life was to ask someone, read a book, watch TV, listen to the radio, talk to people at work, join a club, or go to church and learn from there. Now, the access to information is staggering and wonderful at the same time.

It's been over twenty years now. I do watch TV, but very little. It doesn't dominate my life or my schedule. Now I fight too much other screen time. Too much email, too much social media, too much just browsing on the internet. Getting lost in front of a screen can become an even bigger monster because I can choose from multiple screens.

What affected me the most and what I didn't realize until about ten years later is the enormous amount of brainwashing we experience when we allow our thinking to be exposed to television. Every show, every newscast, and every sitcom are promoting messages, worldviews, and theologies. They are electronic parables, if you will allow me to call them that. Embedded messages are in everything. And almost every-thing on TV has a message that is anti-God, anti-family, and anti-anything-that-is-good-for-us.

My TV viewing formed my worldview. The TV taught me values, theology, morals, and ethics. It was the largest influence in my life. After a steady diet of TV starting in my teenage years, I didn't notice the worldview I was swimming in. But as my thinking transformed from the secular humanism of TV to knowing God and His commandments, precepts, and guidelines of the Bible, I have realized how tricked, duped, and misled I was. I now live in reality and have more face-to-face relationships with real people, not in an electronic medium that distorts reality.

Since your dad was elected to the state House of Representatives over fifteen years ago, we have received an eye-opening education in state government, the history of our state and nation, and reality. It has forced us to seek God more and to seek truth in our situations. His time in the legislature has sobered us to the reality of the day in which we live, which is much different from the world that TV presents. TV is not reality. But for a long time, it was my reality, and as I look back, those were wasted years and a deep shame to me.

Reality is stressful, but the choices to remedy the situations are endless. Less screen time allows me the time to have a fulfilling marriage, fulfilling friendships with other women, a good relationship with all you kids, and most importantly, closer fellowship with God.

So, precious daughter, pay attention to what you fix your eyes on, how much time you spend in front of a screen, and what you are watching on that screen. It is influencing and shaping who you are, affecting your conscience, and forming your worldview.

"Seek the Lord while he may be found; call upon him while he is near; let the wicked forsake his way, and the unrighteous man his thoughts; let him return to the Lord, that he may have compassion on him, and to our God, for he will abundantly pardon. For my thoughts are not your thoughts, neither are your ways my ways, declares the Lord. For as the heavens are higher than the earth, so are my ways higher than your ways and my thoughts than your thoughts" (Isaiah 55:6-9).

13

Mothering

When the word mother is mentioned, most people have strong reactions to it. Whether they were mothered well or poorly, strong feelings about mom are quick to emerge. It is the first bond we long to experience as humans, starting in the womb.

Intentional mothering in our culture has almost become a lost art, at least here in America. When I was in high school in the 1970s, classes in the Fine Arts department such as cooking, sewing, and household budgeting were offered. I took these classes and loved them! They taught me about the basics of life in a succinct, orderly manner, plus they were an easy "A" with no homework, which every student loved.

Granted, not everyone wanted to take these classes, and most were girls, but providing the classes implicitly gave the message to our teenage brains that these things mattered, that the home and what goes on there is important.

But these classes are long gone from the high schools of today, along with the classes that boys liked: wood shop, metal shop, and auto mechanics. Why have the practical classes been sanitized out of the schools? And along with these classes, the art and worthy endeavor of motherhood and fatherhood have been marginalized, pushed to the side, and not given much thought while we go onto "what is really important." To many younger people, their goals are getting a college degree to make a lot of money so they can buy a lot of stuff and travel to exotic places. I know, I know, we have sent all of you kids to college, the military, or you are currently in college, but we have also made it clear to you that college and further education after high school is a means to be educated to support yourself on your way to the higher goals of loving God, serving others, loving your spouse, and if you are blessed to do so, raising kids.

From my vantage point, more women who want to be mothers are realizing its importance in the last ten years or so. (At least, that's my impression.) But overall, since the 1960s and the "sexual revolution", motherhood has been pushed aside by what others have said are more important or weightier matters: careers, self-image, self-fulfillment, and you-don't-need-a-man-to-be-happy. Mothering has been ridiculed in our society

73

in the last fifty years or so. At best, it is largely ignored. At worst, some imply that only women who have not fully developed their brains, skills, and potential are "just" mothers.

I have noticed that a lot of your friends have plans for themselves after high school involving further schooling and career pursuits. At least, that is what they say in public when asked. But when I got to know some of your friends and dug a little deeper, I was elated when I realized that *every* girl had had the priority of the importance and value of children. Some wanted to work with children, mentor children, teach children, have children, or be an influence on children.

This filled me with so much joy that your friends I have the privilege to know value mothering and children, and weren't afraid to admit it. I hope this is only an indication of where our culture is going.

As I was in the process of leaving my job while pregnant with your older brother to go home and be a mom, a guy I worked with asked me if I was going to waste my college education by staying home and "just being a mom." This is the culture we are up against. As if moms do nothing but stay home! Amidst our home priorities and duties, a lot of us are out and about influencing the culture for the good, while making our priority to be physically, mentally and emotionally available for our children.

My beliefs and convictions about mothering come from God and what He says is best for families as described in the Bible. Mothering (and fathering) is the most influential job on the face of the planet, hands down, bar none. The family is the very institution ordained by God in which the world rests. Poet William Ross Wallace (1819-1881) wrote "The hand that rocks the cradle is the hand that rules the world." This is true. The propagation of the species and the future of our world rest on mothering (and fathering). Please always hold the life of a child and motherhood in high regard in your heart and mind, and influence your friends to do so too.

I have found such unexplainable joy and fulfillment in being the mom to you three kids and our godson too. This deep joy can be neither be well described nor found anywhere else. The Bible says children are a blessing from the Lord, and I can witness to this that I am very blessed by being a mother. This is not the message I received after I left home and entered college.

Encouraged to get a degree and pursue a career, I learned very little during my college years about relationships, home and money management, marriage, solving family conflicts, and raising kids. Influenced by adults who said kids should be seen and not heard, and that motherhood was a life of drudgery and wiping dirty noses and bottoms, many women in my group of friends (including myself) were led to believe motherhood ranked right up there with slavery and oppression.

About that time I met some wonderful and inspirational women in the church I was attending. From them I saw that marriage and motherhood, although demanding and exhausting, could also be wonderfully fulfilling and joyful. To be loved by a committed, faithful husband, to have children together and to see him love the kids as much as his wife did were wonderful examples of family and motherhood I saw in families at church. I began to want this for myself.

I'm so glad my view of kids changed over the course of time, and now I understand that children add love, joy, and color to life. Some of my best friends are the mothers of your friends. I would not know most of my friends if it weren't for mothering. Mothers have a bond, a fellowship, a sisterhood.

I haven't even touched on what can and does go wrong when mothers don't mother well, either through their own hurts and shortcomings or because they are too tired or not home. I'm sure you will meet many young men and women who were not parented well, and the spiritual, emotional, and mental damage caused by this will be evident in their adult years. They will either find help and healing in the Christian community, or they will cope with the pain and trauma using drugs, alcohol and a long list of other addictions and vices. Then they will repeat the effects of this trauma onto their own kids. Generational sins are passed down to each successive generation, unless someone decides to stop it.

I hope one day you and your husband, if you are blessed with one, will be blessed by God to be parents, and that you will use the skills, talents, and gifts God has given you to be a mom. Next to loving and respecting your husband, being the best mom you can be will be one of your highest joys. So go ahead and give the talents, skills, and gifts God has given you to motherhood, if that's what you want to do.

While you are a mom, you will not be paid regularly with dollars, but the long-term joy of seeing the fruits of your love and labor in your children far outweighs any dollar amount that you would earn working outside the home. I have found the best joys and values in life cannot be measured in dollars.

My deep prayer is that one day you will be called mother and that in your heart of hearts you will feel the respect and honor that being a mom holds.

You tell me you want a lot of kids. Yay for you! I hope you do have lots of children, that you teach and train them to love God and others, and that you will find the immense joy in raising children that I have found. And I will help you. I will be there for you, talk with you, work with you, be an ear for you, and help you raise your kids, as much as you want me there. You have my full support.

God loves children and the mothers and fathers who bear them. He will give you all of the strength, energy, love, wisdom, knowledge, perseverance, and guidance you need to raise them, if you ask Him. Do your kids a lifelong service by being a good mother. Motherhood matters.

Describing God, Isaiah says, "He will tend his flock like a shepherd; he will gather the lambs in his arms; he will carry them in his bosom, and gently lead those that are with young" (Isaiah 40:11).

14

Obedience

efore I had kids, in my narrow view of life and in my pride, I was the perfect parent. While grocery shopping in college with only myself to feed, I would observe moms of preschoolers pushing carts with naughty kids. I resolved I wouldn't be the mom with the screaming, out-of-control kids. Years later, after you three were born and I was well into diapers and sleep deprivation, I realized I knew very little about being a mother and very little about myself and my own selfishness. I became the mom with the screaming, naughty kids in the grocery cart.

I didn't know how to discipline and train you kids. I was unequipped as a mom of toddlers. I wanted to raise children that would grow up to be wholesome, healthy, right-minded adults, not pests and nuisances to society. Many days I wondered what we would have in the end of this parenting stint, and I severely doubted my ability as a mother. My saying at the time was, "There they go, and I must hurry because I am their mother." That's how I felt much of the time— exhausted, behind, and unorganized. My imagined perfection and now even my adequacy were long gone.

Sometime during your childhood, I realized that I had to get it together so I could stay even one step ahead of you kids. Practically, this meant getting up earlier than you did, setting out breakfast and other morning needs the night before, and thinking ahead about the plan for the next day. This is a small example of my practical efforts at the time to keep it together and have you kids headed in the right direction.

But in my heart, it was another story. I soon began to realize that unless I took care of my own heart issues, I could never lead you kids where you should go. One Sunday at church, the pastor pointed out that we cannot lead someone where we ourselves have never been.

When planning a mountain climbing expedition or travel in a foreign country, smart people find the best guide to lead them. Such a guide has traveled the route many times that they now want to take, knows its features and dangers, and also knows what to take along to make the experience go well. Ever tried to follow people in a work or volunteer situation who didn't know what they were doing or where they were going? It's frustrating.

I realized that if I was the leader and the guide as your mother, I needed to figure out what to do and where I wanted to take you. And this started with myself.

Up until this time, I had let many heart issues go unattended and I realized that if I did not take care of myself first, I would pass on these poor habit patterns and dysfunctional ways to you kids. That scared me. So, out of fear I decided to do the work to change things. A daunting and painful task was before me.

Surprisingly, it started with obedience. As it dawned on me how I might accomplish this mothering mission, I realized that half-hearted attempts or partial determination was not going to cut it. I needed to do this with 100 percent heart and effort, and it began by obeying God in everything.

When we go to school, hold jobs, or perform tasks, we have to do *all* aspects of it well and successfully. We cannot just do what we like and ignore the rest. In school, you don't have the choice to do only the assignments or take only the classes you like. You have to take everything required. To hold a job, you have to do all it needs, not just what is fun or what you prefer. This is what it is like to follow God. I realized I must obey everything He has laid out in His love and mercy for us, not just cherrypick through the commandments I liked, or obey when I felt like it, or when obeying made me feel good. I could not ignore some of what He required and halfheartedly obey only when I wanted to.

I won't lie. This was hard. Human nature is naturally lazy and tries to find the shortcut or the easy road. Why walk when we can ride a bus? Why ride a bus when we can drive a car? We want the easy, quick, comfortable, less painful route in life's tasks.

God puts a very high priority on obedience. He demands it if we want to follow Him. The Bible says that if we love God, we will obey Him. He certainly loves us, and gave us all we need to obey Him. He won't force us to obey, but many pitfalls and dangers await we who do not follow the guide and obey His words and commands. He requires steadfast obedience, and it is our job to give it. It is the one thing we must give God, and He cannot make us obey or give obedience to us. We must do it ourselves.

Often people wonder what they can do for God, and the answer is nothing. He needs nothing from us and is self-sufficient without us. But He wants us. This is the mystery: why does He love us or even bother to give us the time of day, let alone His love letter to us contained in the Bible so we could escape our own sinful choices? This question may never be answered; however, we can give God our obedience.

Obedience, along with sacrifices of praise, are the best things we can give God for through them, all else can happen. The fruit of the Spirit, love, joy, peace, patience, kindness, goodness, faithfulness, gentleness, and self-control are excellent, but those are what God gives us and come out of our obedience. Obedience is what we give Him. Obedience is one of the ways we tell God we love Him.

How do you obey? When you know you should do something, do it. The longer you put it off, the longer you argue with yourself in your head about obeying, the longer it takes to respond, all weaken your resolve to obey. These delay tactics over time make your desire to obey slowly evaporate and make it harder the next time the conviction comes around to obey.

Waiting until you feel like obeying and basing your obedience level on your feelings will rarely result in success. Obedience is a decision, not waiting for a positive thought or impulse causing you to obey. It's a decision of the will, not an action based on feelings.

Now that I have been a mother almost thirty years, I realize that obedience is a lifelong commitment and struggle. It will not come naturally. I am an expert in rationalization and procrastination. But my desire to please Him has become stronger and stronger as I have gotten to know Him, spent time reading the Word, and coming to understand how much He loves us. Therefore, my desire to obey has grown tremendously.

Obedience comes at a high price because we need to stop doing the deeds of darkness, and do deeds of light. In sacrifice, something dies. In obedience, something lives.

We rationalize that obedience is some undesirable task or duty that we must do to fulfill God's commandments or to earn His love. Since I am convinced He knows me intimately, loves me, died for me, and is preparing a place for me in eternity with Him, it is now my desire to want to obey. Obedience to our loving Heavenly Father is now motivated by His love for me, not some duty-bound check list that I must fulfill to be accepted by Him. My obedience now comes out of the relationship I have with Him, understanding His love and care for me, and not before I have understood or trusted Him.

Jesus was the ultimate sacrifice, so we wouldn't have to sacrifice. He provides everything so we can, in obedience, reap what He has already sown. He did all the work of obedience for us. And by obedience to Him and what He says in His Word, we can ultimately reap eternal life.

Obedience is worth it. Although often unpopular and against the flow, it is what leads us to a right relationship to God, and allows us to have peace of mind that we desire. And, it allowed me to lead you where you should go, because I had been there myself. I was now the mother I needed to be because of my obedience.

Jesus says, "If you love me, you will keep my commandments" (John 14:15).

"Do you not know that if you present yourselves to anyone as obedient slaves, you are slaves of the one whom you obey, either of sin, which leads to death, or of obedience, which leads to righteousness? But thanks be to God, that you who were once slaves of sin have become obedient from the heart to the standard of teaching to which you were committed, and, having been set free from sin, have become slaves of righteousness" (Romans 6:16-18).

15

The Bible

*T*he Bible is my favorite book, the love letter from God
to people. Written by men who were inspired by the
Holy Spirit over thousands of years, each little book within the
big book tells a streamlined and consistent message that God
loves us and sent His son Jesus to us so we could further comprehend His love for us, and be reconciled to Him.

This infallible Word of God crosses all cultures, times, and
seasons. It unravels the mystery of who God is, boxing Him in
amongst words, so we can begin to know and understand Him.
It puts the spiritual and impossible into language so this infinite,
perfect, all-knowing, forever God who has no beginning and
no end can communicate with us, mere mortals.

It is the oldest and most verifiable book ever. The Bible
is the only source of absolute divine authority, and it alone
is capable of invading both our minds and hearts for eternal

change. It is the complete and sufficient source of information about every area of life. It stands above all others, this book among books.

One day years ago, my boss sent me to Tacoma to meet with an attorney over some nasty and sticky issues we were dealing with. I wasn't looking forward to the day nor the visit with the attorney.

I pushed the elevator button in the high-rise building and stepped out of the elevator on the top floor and into the impressive law offices. Leather chairs, rich carpeting, and a huge, half-circled, wooden reception desk greeted me. In this expansive reception area, lining two of the walls with floor to ceiling bookshelves were rows upon rows of law books. Hundreds of books, richly bound with titles displayed in gold lettering, stood uniformly in straight rows.

The books were filled with *the law*: property rights law, injury law, environmental law, corporate law, divorce law, medical malpractice law, financial law, intellectual property law, and on and on. The books were filled with some of the laws of our land, written in tiny print on thin paper.

What struck me the most was the sheer number of books, probably over one thousand. I was overwhelmed by these laws, decided by legislation or the courts, which we as people of Washington and the United States must follow.

Later, as I was thinking about this visit to the law office and the multitude of law books I had seen, I thought about God and how the Creator of the universe who made all and knows all and sees all, only used *one* book to explain Himself and His laws to us. God could say it in one book and legislatures, courts, and Congress are still producing laws to define, pin down, and with exact precision decide for us the law.

God, who is much wiser than us, has expressed it all in the Bible. Human beings, who have a darkened understanding, have produced literally thousands of laws and continue to produce more laws.

Are we better off for all of this law producing effort? How could God tell us everything we need in a single book, and we humans are not satisfied and continue to pump out more laws year after year? The Bible speaks plainly about this, and it is not written in the lofty and convoluted language of legalese which is often extremely difficult to understand.

The Bible speaks plainly about God and us humans, and large parts of it are easy to understand. Not that we can comprehend God completely, but we can know and understand what He has said to us in the Bible.

The Bible, Scripture from God, may be only one book, but it is the only book that is 100 percent true and the only book that will endure true to the end. It has drastically impacted my life. I estimate I have read a couple thousand books, not including the hundreds of magazine articles, newspapers, and online news articles: yet the Bible's understanding, wisdom, revelation, and guidance cannot even be touched by all of the other books ever written put together.

Dearest daughter, many things will clamor for your attention. Messages will shout at you, lure you, and entice you away from what is true and real. The best way to understand what is real, refocus, cut through the noise, find your balance, and build a foundation to stand on is to read the Bible and do what it says. Let me save you from a lot of heartache, detours, and dangers from pits dug for you to fall into: read the Bible every day to avoid the snares and traps of life that lie to you, rob you, steal from you, and can eventually kill you.

There are two steps to reading this Book. The first step is to read what it says— read the passages, stories, wisdom, and poetry it has to offer, and familiarize yourself with what it is saying. Know the story, the themes, the points: get the words of the Book into your brain.

The second step is the most vital, and until you do it, the words and message of the Book will remain irrelevant to your life. You must accept what it says. You must digest it, believe it, trust in it, submit to it, act upon it, obey it, and own it.

When we are given a gift, we receive it: but we must accept it, unwrap it, open it up, and own it for it to belong to us. It's the same with the Bible. Ask God to make the words on the page come alive to you by the Holy Spirit, and He will if you submit to them, digest them, believe them, trust in them, obey them, and own them. The words of the Bible will come alive to you by the power of the Holy Spirit, if you accept what it says. God will show up.

Before you begin reading, you can ask God to give you understanding to what He is saying through His Word. It's a simple prayer: "God, please give me understanding as I read Your Word, and help me to know what it is saying." Amen. That's it: a simple prayer. And He speaks to me, and I often understand something that I have never known before, or I feel sharpened and refreshed from His words of truth and love.

No other book will transform and guide you to the One who can heal you. God has spelled out for us who He is, who we are, and what we should do. He has plainly told us about Himself, so we won't have to wonder and guess who God is or what He is like. It takes the guesswork out of wondering who God is and how we should approach Him. Anything spiritual that does not agree and align with the Bible is false.

When I am gone and no longer walk this earth, and you need guidance, support, love, comfort, and help, seek out those godly people who can be for you what you need: but most of all, read the Bible and be guided, supported, loved, comforted, and helped by God through His words. He has allowed Himself to be confined amongst the words of the Bible for us, so we could know who He is, how much He loves us, and how to come to Him and please Him.

It is the Book among books: the final answer; the mystery unraveled. Heaven and earth will pass away, but His words in this powerful and everlasting book will never pass away.

"All Scripture is breathed out by God and profitable for teaching, for reproof, for correction, and for training in righteousness, that the man of God may be competent, equipped for every good work" (2 Timothy 3:16-17).

"Whoever heeds instruction is on the path to life, but he who rejects reproof leads others astray" (Proverbs 10:17).

"My son, if you receive my words and treasure up my commandments with you, making your ear attentive to wisdom and inclining your heart to understanding; yes, if you call out for insight and raise your voice for understanding, if you seek it like silver and search for it as for hidden treasures, then you will understand the fear of the Lord and find the knowledge of God.

91

For the Lord gives wisdom; from his mouth come knowledge and understanding; he stores up sound wisdom for the upright; he is a shield to those who walk in integrity, guarding the paths of justice and watching over the way of his saints. Then you will understand righteousness and justice and equity, every good path; for wisdom will come into your heart, and knowledge will be pleasant to your soul; discretion will watch over you, understanding will guard you, delivering you from the way of evil, from men of perverted speech, who forsake the paths of uprightness to walk in the ways of darkness, who rejoice in doing evil and delight in the perverseness of evil, men whose paths are crooked, and who are devious in their ways" (Proverbs 2:1-15).

Thank you to Rev. Fred Williams of Snohomish Community Church for his notes on his sermon about the Bible, some of which are contained in this chapter.

16

No Delete Buttons in Life

*L*ife has no delete buttons. As you are typing on your computer and make an error, just hit delete or the backspace button, and voila! Your error has vanished. What a relief! What a great invention. However wonderful this may be, this does *not* resemble life.

When we make errors in life, when we make mistakes and say the wrong thing, when we sin against someone, when we sin against God, when we do something that we later regret, it is out there forever. Every sin is against God, and He sees everything, knows everything, understands everything. We cannot erase past actions and redo them over again without God or anyone knowing or remembering the first action or without bearing the consequences of our sin.

It is a huge mistake to think *I will just do this little sin, allow myself to tell this little lie, let that swear word fly, or disobey just once or twice, and no one will notice. It's not hurting me to indulge just this once. It's such a small matter anyway. I will then later ask God to forgive me, and I know He will* and then go on sinning and doing wrong. This is known as "cheap grace," and God does not wink at it or turn a blind eye to it. This is outright disobedience, and we will pay for the consequences of our actions, even though God will forgive us later if we ask Him to.

Forgiveness does not mean He erases the negative consequences of our decisions, although in some instances He may choose to do so in His mercy. Forgiveness from God removes the penalty we must pay for our sins, but it does not remove the consequences.

For example, let's take the popular sin of fornication or sex outside of marriage. A girl of seventeen decides she is going to have sex before marriage and ends up with a venereal disease, a sexually transmitted disease (STD). She suffers the pain and discomfort from this disease, and she may realize later in life when she wants to have a child that it has caused her to be infertile. She later confesses her sin of fornication to God, but the consequences of her poor choice and sin never leave her. God will forgive her of her sin if she asks, and she can be made right before God, but He does not remove the consequences of her actions— the disease she will carry for the rest of her life and her infertility from the disease.

This is an extreme example of my point. But it is true that we will suffer the consequences of our wrong choices, either immediately or in the future. Maybe the consequences will be dulled consciences, damages to relationships, financial penalties, or some other painful results of our sins, but we will still walk through the suffering of our poor choices in the midst of our forgiveness.

This is why it is so important not to sin in the first place. Just to shrug at God's mercy and grace, thinking it's possible to redeem the forgiveness coupon later, is treating Jesus's death on the cross like it was some cheap event. And it shows a poor understanding of the gospel and what God will do and not do for us.

If we lie, we will have to pay for the lies eventually, in spite of being forgiven for the original lie. Yes, Jesus did pay for our sins so we could escape hell and His wrath, but we will all be called into account for our choices, right or wrong, in this life. If we lie, cheat, steal, sin against our bodies, treat others wrongly, drink too much alcohol, and do a host of other wrongs, we will have to live with the consequences of our poor choices.

There are "do overs" with God, but we do something over while living with the knowledge of the past and working through the pain and heartache of it with God at our side. Yes, this is comforting and living in His grace, but wouldn't it be better to not have sinned in the first place if we have a choice? This is why the gospel is so powerful. The blood Jesus shed on the cross as payment for our sins, His death to pay the penalties we deserve for doing wrong and violating His laws and commandments, is so precious and costly. His resurrection gives us power over death, the last enemy of our souls. All this was necessary because we are born sinners and need Him to give us the power over our sins, so we can be free from torment and do what is right.

Yes, life has no delete buttons. My prayer for you is that you choose well the first time and not let your fleshly desires lead you astray. And don't be ashamed and embarrassed to admit you have fleshly desires. We all do. We struggle to live lives of self-control and restraint. It's part of being human. Thus, the reason for the gospel, for it is the power of God for salvation.

"Blessed is the man who remains steadfast under trial, for when he has stood the test he will receive the crown of life, which God has promised to those who love him. Let no one say when he is tempted, 'I am being tempted by God,' for God cannot be tempted with evil, and he himself tempts no one. But each person is tempted when he is lured and enticed by his own desire. Then desire when it has conceived gives birth to sin, and sin when it is fully grown brings forth death" (James 1:12-15).

"Beloved, I urge you as sojourners and exiles to abstain from the passions of the flesh, which wage war against your soul" (1 Peter 2:11).

"For I am not ashamed of the gospel, for it is the power of God for salvation to everyone who believes, to the Jew first and also to the Greek. For in it the righteousness of God is revealed from faith for faith, as it is written, 'The righteous shall live by faith' " (Romans 1:16-17).

"Let marriage be held in honor among all, and let the marriage bed be undefiled, for God will judge the sexually immoral and adulterous" (Hebrews 13:4).

17

Dating Boys

When you begin serious dating I want to tell you about a few guidelines regarding boys—er, uh, I mean young men. Few will be talking about these guidelines in this day of loose boundaries and minimal restrictions on much of moral conduct.

Please hear my heart in what I am trying to say. I only want your best; really, truly, I do. I am not trying to squelch your fun or throw cold water on your feelings. But I don't want you to get hurt. You are not five years old anymore, and I cannot fix your boo-boos with a Band-Aid and a kiss. Choices you make now have life-altering consequences. Please give these suggestions some thought and merit.

Men are attracted to women, but not every man has good motives, nor is he a man of integrity. You will meet two types of men.

The first are men of virtue. Virtuous men protect, guard, and defend women and are kind and considerate to them. The second are self-centered men. Selfish men take, use, abuse, and neglect women, and are harsh and mean towards them.

So how can you know what a guy is like? It takes time.

Here are a few guidelines to get started, a road map if we can call it that.

To start a relationship with a guy off on the right foot, it's best to not call or text him first— or do whatever will be done in the technology superhighway of a culture we live in— first. By the time you read this book, I know you will already have heard this and be beyond some of this advice, but appease me as your mother, and let me put it on paper for your beautiful eyes to read. Allow the guys you want to know better do the initiating and the pursuing.

I can hear your thoughts now and I know that you might be skeptical about what I have to say. What I am saying to you comes from love and compassion for your future relationship. I know your generation is not shy with the opposite sex and can be numb to those things in the culture that are sexually driven. I realize this, but it still does matter to God and *me* that life needs to be lived with boundaries and respect for yourself and others that honor everyone involved. More than likely, every boy and girl you meet will be someone's spouse one day, so think of this as you are interacting with boys and young men.

Our feminine sexuality is precious and powerful. Our ability to lure and attract the opposite sex is a gift from God. How we handle this gift is important. It is a gift to be used wisely and carefully.

Men naturally notice women and much doesn't have to be done for them to notice. God has made men to be visually attracted to women. This is not a design flaw or character weakness. It's how God wired men, and women who know this take the responsibility to respect it and not take advantage of it.

However, teenage girls and women can knowingly or unknowingly exploit this. An immature teenage girl who has spent two hours in front of the mirror and in front of her closet maximizing herself, wearing tight and revealing clothes is not doing herself any favors. The attention she may receive may be pleasing to her in the short term, but in the long-term it probably won't do her any good or gain love and respect. Your natural beauty will shine through as you be yourself. In the long run, it's more about your character than what you wear.

With this in mind, here are some key points to look for when you begin to date. These characteristics are areas of a relationship to think about, but the young man won't necessarily have each of them or meet every one. After you have decided a particular guy appeals to you, think about this general list of characteristics.

- Does he have the character qualities you like? Does he have the raw ingredients for the making of a good man? Think about the character qualities of a guy you'd like to date, and then look for these qualities.

- Is he courteous? Look for a man who opens doors for you, pays for your dates, and calls ahead of time for a date. He should not shy away from face to face conversation with you, hiding behind texts and social media.

- Is he respectful? For example, he should respect his parents and adults in authority over him and talk respectfully to adults. He will often consider your time and give you time to do the things you need to do. He will not insist on having all of your free time.

- Does he have good morals? He should not want to do anything with or to you that is immoral or against God's standards for healthy relationships. This includes having sex, drinking alcohol under twenty-one years of age, smoking dope, taking drugs, or any other law-breaking behavior.

- How does he speak? Does he tell the truth, or does he lie to hide bad behavior? He should not use bad language towards you or around you, either.

- How are his driving habits? When you are in the car with him, you should not feel in danger because of his risky driving habits. And he should *never* drink alcohol and then ask you to ride in a car with him if he is driving! Do not ride in a car with a driver who has been drinking alcohol, because you do not know how much he or she has consumed.

- Does he have a good work ethic? He should be gainfully employed, in college working on a college degree, in the military, learning a trade, or other worthy effort. He should be doing something worthwhile to make himself a better man. He should have the mindset that he wants to be the provider for himself and his future family.

- He is not a woman. Know this. He will never *be* like you. If you are disappointed that he doesn't want to do the things women do, like window shop, fuss over his hair and body, and talk for hours about girl stuff while drinking coffee, realize you are in the company of a man. A good man will try to understand you and be good to you, but he will not *be* like you.

- Does he have convictions and an inner moral code? Does he have self-control or an anger problem? You should not be the object of his anger, and he should not direct his temper at you. He may get heated while he is expressing himself, and I hope you will one day enjoy a man of conviction, but he should not direct his anger at you personally, either verbally or physically.

- How does he handle relationship conflicts? Is he willing to discuss difficult subjects? Or does he run and hide from conflict? If he is not willing to discuss even the small conflicts while dating, realize this will not change as you deepen your relationship and the issues get larger.

- How does he treat women? How does he treat his own mother, sisters, aunts, and grandmothers? Does he respect the women of his family?

- What is the relationship with his father? Has he had good mentoring? Does he have a father? Boys need fathers or father figures.

- Does he have a relationship with God? Does he know God and have devotion and commitment to Him?

When you think you may want to be with him long-term, and through time, conversation, and counsel from people you trust, then allow him bit by bit to go deeper into your heart.

Until this time, guard your heart, for it is the wellspring of life. Do not give your heart away easily. This most often results in a broken heart — yours—and investing your heart in a man prematurely is not wise.

Out there are thousands of awesome young men. It's worth the time to think these things over before you begin to seriously date.

When I started to date your dad, what initially attracted me to him was that he spent long hours at work and had a great work ethic. I knew he was a Christian, but it wasn't until after we were friends for a year and then had our first date that I found out that he was a devoted, genuine Christian who truly did serve God first. What also struck me about him was that when he talked to me, he looked into my eyes and talked to me. He didn't look at my chest when he talked to me or seem hurried to get past the small talk and straight to the physical. He respected me, day and night.

We were friends. This allowed me relax around him, be myself, and not worry about keeping my guard up. Because of this I was more attracted to him.

He also had genuine care and concern for me *and* my friends, since my own father had spent little time with me and didn't know my friends. As a genuinely nice guy, I felt safe to be around him. I was not physically threatened wondering if he was waiting to take my clothes off. He respected me, and we spent fun, bonding times together dating while he did not try to take from me what wasn't his.

One of the best pieces of advice I can give you is marry your friend. The better relationships between husband and wife are those who started out as friends first. Take the time to develop a friendship first.

If your attraction to a guy is only physical, this relationship will not last. Relationships must be more than skin deep to endure. Bodies age, beauty fades, and the irritations and trials of life quickly test relationships. Relationships based in a shared faith in God have vitality, hope and happiness and are not based on the physical.

I am writing this chapter in hopes to prevent heartache for you and to help you discern the motives of men. I have been married for over thirty years and raised two sons and helped raise one godson. I made a lot of poor choices in college when it came to men and dating. Men are not built like us women, nor do they think like we do. Do not make the mistake and assume a man is like a woman. They are different from us, physically, emotionally, and mentally.

I deeply care about you and your well being. I am not trying to cut your fun short or to stifle your life or choices. You will soon discover that young men are appealing, entertaining and awesome to be with—the good ones, anyway. I wish so much that a caring adult would have told me these things when I was young. It would have saved me so much grief and heartache.

We all want close, warm, safe, intimate relationships in our lives. It's worth the time, effort, and skill to learn how to wisely choose whom you want to spend your time with, especially when it comes to young men.

"My son, pay attention to what I say; listen closely to my words. Do not let them out of your sight, keep them within your heart; for they are life to those who find them and health to a man's whole body.

Above all else, guard your heart, for it is the wellspring of life. Put away perversity from your mouth; keep corrupt talk far from your lips. Let your eyes look straight ahead, fix your gaze directly before you. Make level paths for your feet and take only ways that are firm. Do not swerve to the right or the left; keep your foot from evil" (Proverbs 4:20-27 NIV).

18

Temptations — *H.A.L.T.*

*W*hat is temptation? According to The American
Dictionary of the English Language from 1828,
written by Noah Webster, it is "The act of tempting; enticement to evil by arguments, by flattery, or by the offer of some
real or apparent good." It is also described as "Solicitation of
the passions." Juicy stuff.

Temptation is the enticement to do evil, but it is not sin. Sin
is acting on the enticement, carrying out the evil. Temptation
is the invitation to sin by our own flesh, from the invitation of
others, or by the devil himself. But only if we act on the temptation does it then become sin. If you are tempted but haven't
followed through on it, you have not sinned.

How do you resist temptations that you will face and live a
life pleasing to God? To give you strength to resist temptations,
there are four issues to pay attention to. How you are feeling

and what frame of mind you are in may make you more vulnerable to temptations.

The four things that need answers when you are facing temptations follow the acronym "HALT".

Ask yourself, are you:

- **Hungry.** If you are hungry, you tend to not think clearly. Your blood sugar may be low and you feel drained. Foggy brains make decisions harder when you are hungry. Often after eating some good food, unmanageable problems seem smaller and more manageable. Our will power increases if we are fed nutritious food.

- **Angry.** If you have unresolved anger at something or someone, your emotions may take over and your reasoning is poor. Anger distorts our view of reality. Figure out why you are angry and solve it, or at least put it aside until you can deal with the problem later.

- **Lonely.** If you are isolated, and not in a group of other girls or supportive friends and adults who know you, it can leave you vulnerable to temptations. Birds fly in flocks, and cattle move in herds. There is a reason for this: safety from predators, and for us humans, they are often predators of the mind and heart.

- *Tired.* When we are tired, we give in to things more easily and may not have the will to endure or fight off temptations. Fatigue distorts reality, fogs our brains, and weakens our resolves to do what we know is right.

If you answer "yes" to any of the above, realize you are not at your best, and do something about it. It's okay to say no to things making time for yourself and solving one or more of the above problems. Saying no to a late party on Friday night may be the better choice for your moral and physical health.

You've answered the "HALT" questions, now how will you handle temptations? I suggest you have a plan *before* you venture out, go to a party, go out on a date, attend college, or whatever else you will do in life, and decide now how you will handle these situations, big or small. When you have your right mind about you is the best time to make decisions, instead of waiting until you are faced with an immediate decision or in the heat of the moment. Decide early to guard your heart and establish your boundaries. The goal is to try to avoid being caught off guard and then making poor decisions.

Avoiding temptation will be a lifelong fight. Temptations do not reduce in frequency or duration as you age. I wish they did. Temptations will be something you deal with your whole life.

How can you put yourself in a position to overcome temptations?

- Read the bible every day. Yes, we can rely on our own strength and will power, but this soon wanes and needs sharpening, refreshing, and rejuvenation.
- Pray and ask God for strength.
- Think ahead, plan ahead, anticipate what may be coming your way. Be alert. I do this by looking at my calendar and responsibilities, see what's coming, and giving these things forethought and planning.
- Find a small group of like-minded girlfriends at each phase of life. There are myriads of small groups. It's best to have a social group of supportive friends.
- Pay attention to your body and your emotions. Ask yourself the "HALT" questions: are you hungry, angry, lonely, or tired? If so, take action to do something about it.

You'll face temptations just as Jesus did during moments of physical, spiritual, or emotional weakness. You can overcome them if you take the time to prepare yourself now, give them some thought before they are staring you in the face, and most importantly, pray and stay close to Jesus. The key is to prepare yourself ahead of time as much as possible, anticipate what's coming, and to reduce surprises and impulsive decisions, to avoid giving in to temptation.

"No temptation has overtaken you that is not common to man. God is faithful, and he will not let you be tempted beyond your ability, but with the temptation he will also provide the way of escape, that you may be able to endure it" (1 Corinthians 10:13).

19

American Idols

When a certain TV show with a similar name became popular a while ago, I cringed the first time I heard the title. Enamored with fame, this generation is quick to idolize those amongst us with talent, skills, and abilities that sound and look good on a stage.

Who invented music? God did. Why would He invent such wonderful sounds to capture our attention, convey a message, draw us in, and set our mood? So we would worship Him with it. In the meantime, now for multiple seasons, millions clamor to see who will become the next famous winner of the show and the next American to fawn over.

Idolatry is something that the Bible has been addressing since the beginning. The human heart has had a problem with idols since the beginning starting with Adam and Eve. God says we are to have no idols and said this in the first and second commandments He gave us. The first four commandments of the Ten Commandments define how we are to have a relationship with God, and the other six are how we are to not conduct ourselves with others.

Every person wants to worship someone or something. God created us with "God-shaped vacuums" in our souls, and these vacuums can only be filled by His Son, Jesus Christ. Oh, of course, millions try and fill them with lots of other things, which can be considered idols— fame, fortune, money, power, popularity, false religions, sex, drugs, success, celebrities, selfish ambitions— the list is endless. None of these things will ever satisfy the longings of human hearts, but these are the idols people use to replace Jesus.

Most people would not admit to serving idols, as the word is not common amongst us in the twenty-first century, except when everyone is exclaiming about this TV show. Other words besides *idol* to describe what I am explaining to you could be *addiction, obsession, fixation*, or what drives us consuming our hearts and energies. Idols are what people live for and seek if they are not living for and seeking God.

The problem with being swept away in the river of the cultural idols is that they become our internal compasses, unless we resist and fight them. These internal compasses then affect our decisions, determine our paths, and have great influence on where we end up in life— or don't end up. The internal compasses inside us determine where we go and how we get there.

Because I am born again, the Spirit of the living God living inside of me guides my conscience that it is wrong to have idols, no matter how harmless they may appear, and no matter how frequently so many willingly follow them. The tsunami of the cultural idols will pull us out to sea and spiritually drown us, unless we are prepared, see them coming, and fight them with everything in us to resist.

Moses was hardly out of their sight before the Israelites had built a golden calf as an idol while he was talking to God on the mountain receiving the Ten Commandments. So they settled for a golden cow they had made from their jewelry and trinkets instead of the words directly from God.

The world exalts idols and makes them really big and important. They are seen and exalted by everyone who worships the idols. But in Christ, we realize God is really big and important. He is not naturally seen, and those who do not worship the idols are misunderstood. I hope you realize that this chapter is not about a TV show. TV is only my illustration to make the point that idols still fill our landscapes.

May you grow and mature to listen to the Spirit of the living God inside of you so you can resist these idols, and teach your teenage daughter should you be blessed to have one, how wrong it is to uphold and be enamored with idols.

Deuteronomy 5:7-21 lists the Ten Commandments. God says:

1. You shall have no other gods before me (v.7).
2. You shall not make for yourself a carved image (v.8).
3. You shall not take the name of the Lord your God in vain (v. 11). [No swearing using God's name or His son's name.]
4. Observe the Sabbath day to keep it holy (v. 12).
5. Honor your father and your mother (v. 16).
6. You shall not murder (v. 17).
7. You shall not commit adultery (v. 18).
8. You shall not steal (v. 19).
9. You shall not bear false witness against your neighbor (v. 20). [No lying.]
10. You shall not covet your neighbor's wife... or anything that is your neighbor's (v. 21).

20

Don't Judge Me. Be Tolerant.

*W*hen people discuss a controversial subject and one person brings in God or Scripture to shed light on the matter, the opposing party usually says, "Don't judge me!" This is supposed to end the discussion.

Being nonjudgmental, tolerant, and accepting of every lifestyle is supposed to be the highest law of the land. We who have biblical convictions are supposed to stop talking and go away because this standard of being nonjudgmental rules the day.

As I have ventured out in youth culture, I have stated that practicing homosexuality is wrong. I say this not because I am an expert or that my opinion matters in weighty subjects but because that is what the Bible says. But some feel what God has said is unacceptable. I have carefully addressed this subject with as much gentleness and careful wording as I could muster, but as expected, someone cried with "Don't judge me! We should all be loving and nonjudgmental towards everyone."

Judging someone is seen as the ultimate no-no, and if the non-judgers were honest, being judgmental is their definition of the ultimate sin in America today. Their definition of tolerance is to be nonjudgmental and to have no boundaries or rules for moral behavior. Those with a biblical value system are supposed to abandon their beliefs and make no statements about immoral lifestyles, even when what they say is said with love and grace. We quickly realize that tolerance only goes one way, but if tolerance is truly tolerance, shouldn't it go both ways?

To be tolerant, those who respect God and His commandments are supposed to abandon those beliefs and move towards those who object to such beliefs. Somehow tolerance never means that those individuals, who want no boundaries on sexuality and sexual behavior, need to move towards a more respectable value system. We who believe the Bible are supposed to abandon our values to move towards *them* to be tolerant.

Dear precious daughter, since we've had a couple of conversations about this, let me clarify for you, as your bigoted mom (as I have been labeled by the left), what we can and cannot judge.

If we judge others on these important matters, is this wrong? Is it a sin to be judgmental? What does the Bible say about judging others?

To get to the point, yes, we are to judge others. But what to judge is carefully explained in Scripture. And when to speak or not to speak about the conclusions we have drawn while judging others is also explained.

As Jesus addressed his disciples, he said, "Judge not, that you be not judged. For with the judgment you pronounce you will be judged, and with the measure you use it will be measured to you. Why do you see the speck that is in your brother's eye, but do not notice the log that is in your own eye? Or how can you say to your brother, 'Let me take the speck our of your eye,' when there is the log in your own eye? You hypocrite, first take the log out of your own eye, and then you will see clearly to take the speck out of your brother's eye" (Matthew 7:1-5).

Notice that Jesus is talking to his disciples, those who believe in Him and are following Him. He is addressing His own. These verses apply to those who follow Jesus, who claim Him, who belong to Him. But Jesus also proclaims these words, "Everyone then who hears these words of mine and does them" (Matthew 7:24) can be a disciple of Jesus if they choose to be.

As I understand from these verses, we are to check our own hearts and motives, admit our faults, repent of and give up any wrong or sin we see in ourselves, and come clean before God. It means we are not to quickly judge fellow believers, but to first judge ourselves soberly and check our motives and actions. Humbling ourselves before God, we are to confess our sins and wrongdoings to Him, while remembering to have an attitude of humility towards Him and others during the whole process.

After we have confessed our own sins to God and received the forgiveness in Jesus Christ, then we are given permission to "take the speck out of our brother's (and sister's) eye." We can then gently and lovingly speak into the lives of our brothers or sisters when it is appropriate to do so.

If we have certain weaknesses or sins we easily fall into, we can often become the biggest judges on this matter in others. So yes, we can judge each other amongst the body of believers, those who fear God, believe in the God of the Scriptures, and who love His Son Jesus Christ.

What about those outside the church, outside the body of believers, and those who claim not to be God-fearing? We are to judge their "fruit." Again, Jesus is addressing his disciples in these next verses.

"Beware of false prophets, who come to you in sheep's clothing but inwardly are ravenous wolves. You will recognize them by their fruits. Are grapes gathered from thorn bushes, or figs from thistles? So, every healthy tree bears good fruit, but the diseased tree bears bad fruit. A healthy tree cannot bear bad fruit, nor can a diseased tree bear good fruit. Every tree that does not bear good fruit is cut down and thrown into the fire. Thus you will recognize them by their fruits" (Matthew 7:15-20).

Let me explain. False prophets are those who claim to speak the truth and teach what God has said, yet teach a lie. They are not disciples, although they often masquerade as such. Teaching others, they are attempting to mislead them by saying their authority to teach and say these things is from God, or from some other authority.

A good example of false prophets are these "experts" who have been brought on to your college campus and have spoken in the lecture series titled, "Two Christian Perspectives on What the Bible Says about Sexual Orientation" that sounds like they are teaching truth from the Bible, but they are false prophets, claiming that practicing homosexuality can be reconciled with Scripture and be acceptable to God.

We will recognize truth tellers by their fruit. Spiritually healthy people bear good fruit, and spiritually unhealthy people bear bad fruit. Sinful persons who want to speak for God cannot bear good fruit, because they want to urge others to agree with them to appease their own consciences and validate their own sins, while leading others astray. And, in the end, if they do not repent and give up their wrongdoings and wrong beliefs, they will be "cut down and thrown into the fire," meaning God will eventually silence them and send them to hell, the place they have chosen due to their lack of repentance. The Bible says these people "are perishing, because they refused to love the truth and so be saved" (2 Thessalonians 2:10).

We are to judge those who speak to us, or by their words and deeds, and to compare it with Scripture. After a careful examination of their words and beliefs about the homosexual lifestyle, we can clearly see they are false prophets.

And we are to do this throughout our lives on all subjects, testing and examining the fruit in others' lives to see if they are telling the truth or telling lies. If you ever wonder if someone is telling the truth, examine their lives, their actions, and their work. Judge them by their fruit.

We are not to judge people's motives or the intents of their hearts, but we certainly are to judge their work, their deeds, and their actions. On the floor of the House of Representatives here in Washington State's capitol, the Speaker of the House will gavel members on the floor who impugn others, members who dispute the truth, validity, or honesty of others' motives. But the Speaker does not gavel members who speak of the words, deeds, or actions of others. By the way, if members are gaveled, their microphones are shut off at that moment. Expected to sit down, they are no longer allowed to speak or finish their speech.

So, on the House floor the Speaker has rules regarding examining the fruit, judging deeds and actions (which is allowed) versus judging motives and intents (which is not allowed). Following the commands of scripture, they have a biblical definition of judging, and don't even realize it. The many liberals on the left who have been in charge of the House for twenty years are living by and enjoying the commands of Jesus yet continually attempt to subvert His ways. Truth seems to permeate its way into everything.

We cannot judge people's motives or intentions. We cannot see into their hearts to understand what they mean or what they intend to do. We are not to judge their hearts, however "for out of the abundance of the heart the mouth speaks" (Matthew 12:34). Their intent and beliefs spill out as they talk and reveal their hearts to us. We can see and eventually judge their fruit by their words and deeds.

Then, how do you know if you should tell people the truth about something wrong? When is it appropriate to speak out and tell people the truth according to Scripture? Here's the rub. I cannot tell you when or how to do this, precious daughter.

This is up to you. Sometimes, after much prayer, Bible reading, and discussion with others that you trust, God will prompt you to tell them in love what conclusions you have made. And sometimes you will need to remain silent and use the judgment you now possess as a matter of prayer between you and God. This decision to speak or not to speak is often troubling and difficult to make.

In our culture today, I observe that a lot of Christians remain silent when they should speak up. These armchair critics remain hidden in their homes or in the pews, in silent safety, not wanting to put themselves out there in the fight. I understand this. Who wants to invite stress, hardships, and insults into their lives? But I believe that marriage, family, and the well being of the kids in our nation are currently in a lot of trauma, crisis, and decay because those with the knowledge of the truth remain silent.

Your dad and I have spent much of our lives telling the truth to our community and state. I won't lie when I say at times this has been costly. But our God of love and mercy has met us in every handshake, conversation, and meeting. He has sustained and revived us after painful and brutal encounters. He has comforted us after painful losses, and given us rest after times filled with pressure, stress, and dread. But also surprisingly, many people have reacted with warmth and acceptance, and buoyed us with their words of encouragement and their faithful prayers. He will do the same for you.

To summarize, we are to lovingly help other believers with their sins and shortcomings but only after we have judged ourselves, repented of our sins, and gotten rid of them in our own lives. Then, with love and humility, compassion and understanding, we can help others.

We are to judge everyone by their fruit. We are not to judge their intents or motives, which we cannot see, but we most certainly can judge their words, deeds, and actions, which we can see. You will know a tree by its fruit. Abandon the tolerance of bad fruit. You be the judge.

21

What Career Should You Choose?

s I discussed in the first letter when I advised that you should clean the kitchen every day as a step to achieving your dreams, another nagging and pressing question you are asked frequently during these high school years is "What are you going to do for a career?" or "What do you want to major in when you go to college?"

This is such a troubling and unfair question in my opinion, because the world is asking you something that you have not begun to figure out yet. You just learned to drive a car and cannot even keep your room clean yet. Your biggest concern is how to get rid of your acne and what you are wearing to the Friday night football game.

In early adulthood, many realize they must earn money, pay the rent, possibly own a car that needs insurance, gas, and tires, and buy their own food to eat. None of these pressing demands have even crossed your mind, and the adults in your life are asking what you want to be when you grow up. Comical questions for such a young girl!

Many parents have cursed their children with the permission to remain in perpetual adolescence into their young adult years, and as you know we have not made it easy for any of you kids to do that. Many parents do not require their kids to grow up and face the realities of adulthood. Your Dad and I have paid the price to be your parents and not your friends, at least while you are still in the home, though we realized a long time ago that all of you kids would bristle at this and not like it. A couple of you kids have said, "You and Dad have set the bar so high." Yes, we did it for your own good and have not asked you to do anything or achieve any goal that you were not capable of.

When you were in high school in between the lands of childhood and adulthood, your mind wanted the independence and freedom of adulthood, but you were incapable of earning enough money to sustain yourself and lacked the mental and spiritual disciplines to keep your life in enough order for happiness or success.

So how do you know what you want to do when you grow up? As you know, we have already discussed this for a long time, but because you are not fully alert to the hopes and plans we have for you, here is what we have done.

Since you were young, we have observed what your natural strengths and talents are, what activities you are drawn to and how you communicate, and we have made an effort to develop and enhance these attributes and proclivities in you. We did this for your brothers also. We are all born with God-given strengths and talents and we have raised you according to Scripture.

"Train up a child in the way he should go; even when he is old he will not depart from it" is stated in Proverbs 22:6. This "in the way he should go" in the original Hebrew language in which it was written means in a child's natural "bent" or ways. So we have made an intentional effort to encourage and nurture you in your natural strengths.

We hold marriage and family in high regard, so I have also encouraged you to pick a career that will be compatible and friendly to marriage and family. I know some careers are more compatible than others to support this, but since you are young and have a choice, I suggest this important detail be part of your decision-making process. Keep the priorities of marriage and home in the mix when you are choosing a money-making job or career.

Today, women are encouraged to chase careers and climb corporate ladders, sacrificing other areas of their lives to do so. Few will admit what this does to their emotional and mental health, as well as marriage and family life. Rare is the woman who only wants a career and nothing else. Most also want to be married to a good man and have children. Studies show that most women want children at some point, so it's best to choose a career that will enable you to balance both home and work. And now that you are blessed with a computer, your work choices are almost endless because you are sometimes able to work remotely from home. I did not have this option while raising kids, and computers now present a whole new challenge of life/work balance. Because you do live in an electronic world, working from home is now a wonderful option for you.

Many more jobs offer a part-time option or the employer allows flexibility in the hours you work while having young kids at home. Don't worry about what should you be when you grow up. Just start working at the obvious entry-level jobs doing something that you like, and go from there. Remember that no one starts with an awesome job. Those who get a lot of satisfaction and enjoyment from their current job did not start there. They arrived after a long period of time working their way there with patience and perseverance.

The Bible expressly states that a man should provide for his family, and this largely means financially. But even if you want to be married to a man who is the primary breadwinner, it is important that you are able to earn money also.

What if your husband breaks his leg or gets seriously ill and is unable to work? Or, heaven forbid, what if he dies and leaves you to manage the home and bills yourself? Many women also face the ugly and painful situation of divorce. So while you are young and have a choice, you need to get training or a college degree in a marketable skill that can earn you some money.

Side note: Our culture today encourages girls to go to college or pursue further education enabling you to get a good-paying job so you can support yourself, regardless of whether you are married or not. I agree with this to a point, because who knows how long you will be single? What if that right guy doesn't come along for a long time? It is important not only to work, but also to have a long-range plan.

In Genesis, when Eve bit the apple and thus began the Fall, God cursed the ground (hence the weeds we now have to pull and the struggles to keep animals alive, among other problems) and the pain that came upon Adam was the life-long toil to work the ground. This "work the ground" represents work outside the home to provide food and other necessities for his family.

God told Eve that in pain she would bring forth children. So the "pain" of what Adam would spend his life and energy doing would be to work by the sweat of his face, and the "pain" of what Eve would spend her life doing was bearing children. Here the main tasks are laid out for male and female. God has wired a man to protect and provide for his wife and family. We women are designed to bear children and be nurturers. If you do get married one day, I encourage you to allow your husband to be the primary breadwinner. It will free you from the mental worry of having to both work outside the home and raise kids. I don't believe God designed nor intended us women to be responsible for both at the same time. For the first ten years, I was home with you kids and did not work outside the home. I barely had enough sanity and energy for that!

When you are in the childbearing years, I recommend reducing or eliminating outside-the-home work hours so you can give your best energy to your husband, home, and kids. Give your husband respect and trust and allow him to fulfill his God-given duty to work for you and your kids. Many women have been hurt by a man because they trusted him to do this and he failed. Give your husband the gift of respect and trust, let him do what he was wired to do, and give yourself the permission to take a break from your outside job to devote yourself to your marriage and kids.

So, what does choosing a career or job look like? How should you get started? What major in college should you choose or what training should you seek? Well, we will discuss this together as life unfolds, but I will encourage you to do something that interests you *and* has moneymaking potential. The goal for vocational training or attending college is to gain a set of skills to earn money. Attending college is not to randomly learn about subjects you are interested in: do that on the internet. College and further training after high school should be for the purpose to gain knowledge and skills that will equip you to earn money.

Personality tests can help you see your strengths and talents and know your natural bent. Also, talent evaluations and aptitude tests can help to guide you. These also can be in the mix as you decide what to do to earn money.

A word of caution: People may encourage you to pursue your passion and to find a job that can completely fulfill you every day in every way, bringing bliss and inner contentment. This job will be the outpouring of your inner passions and desires and will fulfill every vein in your body, every breath of your lungs. It will be your calling, your life's passion and your inner fulfillment, this job full of wonder and joy. It will give you sheer delight to get out of bed each morning and will give you euphoric feelings of accomplishment each year. It will be the answer to your "why" and the reason you were born. And, if you work hard enough at these inner yearnings, it will give you complete fulfillment.

But this is *not* true. Yes, you should find that money-making endeavor that agrees with your natural strengths and abilities and that you generally enjoy, but to assume that somehow this job will be your entire fulfillment and joy is just too much of a stretch. Every job I have had and each woman I have talked to who has a job has expressed a wide range of emotions and levels of fulfillment that go with it. No money-making job on the planet will completely fulfill you. Only Jesus can do that. To place this lie upon your soul that a job is your fulfillment and the entire reason you have for living is a grave mistake. It puts your hope and joy in the wrong place. And if you no longer are employed, does this then reduce your worth as a person and your value to society? Of course not.

Keep the balance of relationships, home, and work, realizing that the important things in life are not measured in dollars. The Westminster Shorter Catechism completed in the year 1647 says it so well. "Man's chief end is to glorify God, and to enjoy him for ever." We are put on this planet to worship God and to love and serve others, while remembering that those whom have received forgiveness from God through Jesus Christ have our glorious and final destination in heaven.

Pursue what you are naturally drawn to. Find that job that can earn you some money. Realize that some jobs are not fun. They humble you in many ways and are just a lot of work. Realize jobs can cut into your fun, sleep, and time for relationships. Remember that you have that job to earn money and to provide a product or service to someone else. Hopefully, you can find some joy and fulfillment in it, but do not expect it will be the end all, final joy you are seeking. And if you keep at it, practice good work skills over the long haul, switch jobs as needed and continue to work, you may eventually have a job that you truly like. Or you may resolve that the purpose of your job is to earn money, and your priority is to find happiness and fulfillment in something else or in a combination of things.

We live in the most amazing, opportunity-filled nation on earth. Develop your skills, and search for a job that can earn you money. But please remember, precious daughter, to always put your hope and trust in God, not in your own strength, talents, job, or money-making abilities. Only in God will you be truly fulfilled, even on your way to earning money.

The Bible gives an amazing description of a good woman. Proverbs 31, starting in verse 11, begins to describe her.

"The heart of her husband trusts in her, and he will have no lack of gain. She does him good, and not harm, all the days of her life. She seeks wool and flax, and works with willing hands. She is like the ships of the merchant; she brings her food from afar. She rises while it is yet night and provides food for her household and portions for her maidens. She considers a field and buys it; with the fruit of her hands she plants a vineyard... She perceives that her merchandise is profitable... She opens her hand to the poor and reaches out her hands to the needy... She makes linen garments and sells them... She opens her mouth with wisdom, and the teaching of kindness is on her tongue. She looks well to the ways of her household and does not eat the bread of idleness" (Proverbs 31: 11-16, 18, 20, 24, 26-27).

This woman figured out how to honor God, do her husband good, bring food from far and wide, work, earn money, sell profitable merchandise, buy real estate, plant a vineyard, make and sell clothing, feed her family and others outside of her family, bless the poor, and not be idle. Surely we can accomplish some of this! We need to work towards something. Work is good for us.

22

Finding Happiness and Joy

On the heels of the work and career chapter, I thought I should follow up with how I have found happiness and joy. I think by now most of what I have written has explained it, but I want to say a few more things about happiness and joy and how to find them.

First of all, what are the definitions of happiness and joy? You won't find these definitions in the dictionary; I have formed these on my own over the years through reading and experience.

Happiness is that good feeling of relief from pain, from gaining what is desired, or finding that love relationship with a man that we women desire. It is getting a new car, new clothes, or a new whatever that we have wanted. It is being free from bother or irritation. Happiness is an emotional pleasure of a good feeling. It is being released from hassle and inconvenience. It is circumstantial, and can ebb and flow, come and go, and be up or down depending upon our circumstances. It is conditional on what is happening around us and to us. It is the feeling we experience when our wants are met and our circumstances are agreeable. It is what is happening to us at the time and whether or not we like it. It often depends upon our emotions at the moment.

Happiness is based on how people are treating us, and whether or not we like it. It is being free from emotional, mental, or physical pain, and the pursuit of this happiness is desired and declared for America in our Declaration of Independence from Great Britain. We think we have a right to it. Those who misunderstand happiness often try and demand others provide it for them.

Joy, on the other hand, is a whole other matter. It is biblical from the beginning, and without God you cannot find joy. Joy is that good, deep-down fact of our deliverance from pain, from gaining the freedom of the heart and soul we desire, of having our sins forgiven and our wrongs erased. It is realizing that our names are written in the Lamb's Book of Life and cannot be erased or blotted out. It is finding and cultivating relationships that we desire based in God. Gaining material possessions does not produce it, although that can be part of our needs fulfilled or our desires met.

Joy is possible in the midst of bother and irritation, because we know our real joy is found in God and what He has done for us, not in how we are feeling. Joy is a choice to see the good, even in the midst of the bad. Joy is not a feeling, although it can be accompanied by good feelings.

Joy often is accompanied by emotional pleasure, but it can also be experienced without it. Joy is not circumstantial and is not conditional on what is happening around us and to us. It is based on the facts of the Bible, knowing God and believing what He says about us and remembering these facts.

It can be had even when our wants are not met and our circumstances are not agreeable. Regardless to what is happening to us at the time, we can choose joy, realizing that this too shall pass and knowing that God has us in His hands.

If others are treating us well or poorly and whether or not we like it, we can still seek God and remind ourselves of His immense love for us. We realize that what He has said about the future will be the final word.

In the midst of emotional, mental, or physical pain, even though we need God and others at this time to help us, we can still find joy because joy is not a feeling. It is a choice to remember how good God is to us, despite our temporary circumstances. No one else can give us joy or take it away from us. Joy is a gift from God.

I realize what I am saying is hard. I fail so often to stop and choose the joy that is mine. I often get caught up in the happiness pursuit, thinking once my situation changes or I am free from my ringing ears and neck pain that I will feel better, and yes, I will feel better. I have tried so much of my life to be healed from emotional and mental pain and have visited many doctors to be free of my physical pain. But I am learning that this freedom from bother and pain is not the source of my joy. I can still have joy in the midst of my physical, mental, and emotional pain.

"The fruit of the Spirit is love, *joy*, peace, patience, kindness, goodness, faithfulness, gentleness, self-control; against such things there is no law" (Galatians 5:22-23). Fruit is eaten after planting the vine or tree, fertilizing it, watering it, tending it, and waiting for it to grow and ripen. We can do this in our spiritual lives. After a lot of years of spending time with God, some of this fruit is now in my life. And one of these is joy.

Joy is not granted by anyone but God. We should not wait for happiness or luck to find us, for happiness is circumstantial, and there is no such thing as luck; but joy can be had by anyone, anywhere, no matter the situation or circumstance.

So, of course, I suggest pursuing happiness, but also choosing joy. Happiness will come and go depending on the outward circumstances, and it is okay to enjoy the good things that happen to us and even find immense pleasure in them. But remember to claim the joy that is yours, joy will last forever because it depends upon the everlasting words of God that will never pass away.

I hope you have a lot of happiness in your life, and I also hope you realize the joy that is yours because we belong to Jesus.

"You make known to me the path of life; in your presence there is fullness of joy; at your right hand are pleasures forevermore" (Psalm 16:11).

"Therefore, since we are surrounded by so great a cloud of witnesses, let us also lay aside every weight, and sin which clings so closely, and let us run with endurance the race that is set before us, looking to Jesus, the founder and perfecter of our faith, who for the joy that was set before him endured the cross, despising the shame, and is seated at the right hand of the throne of God" (Hebrews 12:1-2).

"Count it all joy my brothers, when you meet trials of various kinds, for you know that the testing of your faith produces steadfastness" (James 1:2).

"And the angel said to them, "Fear not, for behold, I bring you good news of great joy that will be for all the people. For unto you is born this day in the city of David a Savior, who is Christ the Lord" (Luke 2:10-11).

"Though you have not seen him, you love him. Though you do not now see him, you believe in him and rejoice with joy that is inexpressible and filled with glory, obtaining the outcome of your faith, the salvation of your souls" (1 Peter 1: 8-9).

23

Trouble

I must teach you something that is rarely spoken or taught. The unpleasant side of life is often unexplained, pushed to the side and ignored, hoping it will somehow go away. It doesn't, and I want to help you walk through it.

In this country of bounty and excess at every level, this is not what is popular or even wanted. I have sat through literally thousands of sermons on Sunday mornings, and pastors have touched on this but never really revealed what is behind the curtain. It's often too hard and too painful to admit, let alone discuss.

In this world, you will live in, be confronted with, and abide with constant trouble. Jesus warns us about it. He says, "I have said these things to you, that in me you may have peace. In the world you will have tribulation. But take heart; I have overcome the world" (John 16:33).

Directly from the mouth of Jesus, He tells us in this life we will have trouble. Often we read this and say, "Yeah, yeah, I know once in awhile we will encounter a difficulty, a loss, or a tragedy. But isn't life mostly good? And if God is so loving and good, He will keep trouble and hard times away from me most of the time. Those who have bad things happen to them, lose jobs, get in car wrecks, lose their money, lose their health, or have someone do something really bad to them must have asked for it or aren't really smart enough to avoid trouble."

If we encounter months or years of pain, suffering, heartaches, and losses, we get discouraged and assume nothing much seems to go our way. We then say of God, "How can a loving God who promises to heal allow this tragedy and pain in my life? Doesn't He love me? If He loved me, wouldn't He remove this from my life or fix it?" We then take our anger out on God because we don't want nor like the trouble and pain we are in.

We assume that pain-free, trouble-free lives are God's blessing on us, and a life of troubles and heartaches are because God hasn't given us what we want, and He is ignoring us and not giving us what we think we need or what will give us relief.

We have completely missed the point, misunderstood what God has said, and translated the words of Jesus through our own darkened misunderstanding and twisted culture. This life of pain and disappointment, sorrow and loss is not the life of wealth and ease that we are told we should expect in America.

In this life, you are promised, guaranteed, and will live in a constant state of trouble. When you get up in the morning, your attitude should be, *In this constant state of trouble, heartache, and pain, I will look for God and His goodness, and I will seek the healing and protection God is offering me this day. Even though trouble, darkness, and fear surround me, and many things will go wrong today and be hard, I know God will rescue me and be with me. I will give God my heart, and obey and follow Him with all of the strength He will give me as I humbly ask Him. And I will expect Him to meet me in my pain and heartache, disappointment and loss, and then I will rejoice and be thankful for the mercy and grace He will give to me. I expect trouble this day but will look for God who is always with me because I gave Him my heart and life, and He promises to never leave me. He will deliver me from this present trouble, darkness, and fear, and because of that, I can be joyful today."*

But instead we are taught to think and believe, *I hope this day is awesome! I wonder what good will come to me today? Maybe I will receive an unexpected check in the mail or find a wad of cash! I hope nothing bad happens and that my circumstances run smoothly because I don't want any more pain or trouble to happen to me. I hope everything goes well, with no bumps in the road, and my irritating boss will finally change his behavior and be nice to me. I hope I ace all my tests at school and they are easy. I hope that everyone I talk to will be nice today. I sure hope my husband/friends/relatives will be happier today and that my kids will behave today and do nothing wrong. I wish I could lose weight without eating a healthy diet and exercising. Wouldn't that be awesome? I sure wish I could throw responsibility to the wind and do nothing today but watch movies and go shopping!"* And on and on it goes, believing in this falsely happy life we hope one day will fall into our laps.

God is good, loving, and just. But we do have an enemy of our souls, the devil. Jesus says of this devil, named Satan, "He was a murderer from the beginning, and has nothing to do with the truth, because there is no truth in him. When he lies, he speaks out of his own character, for he is a liar and the father of lies" (John 8:44).

I believe the devil has lied to us because he is the father of lies, and we have unknowingly believed him. We have believed the devil's lies that if life is smooth and carefree, God loves and blesses us. If we have trouble, pain, and sorrow, God doesn't love and bless us. But if we read the words of Jesus *and* believe Him, He tells us plainly that we will have trouble and that has nothing to do with whether He loves us or not. This world is not our home, and we are strangers and aliens here. This is why we do not feel at home here and why something is missing. We wish for the struggle to stop. We are longing for heaven, where God will put it all right and where our struggles will be over. What a fabulous day that will be!

In the meantime, so many people are mad at God and blame Him for their troubles, when they should be mad at Satan and blame him for much of the sorrow, heartache, and loss we experience. The god (little "g") of this world, the devil, has a mission that Jesus told us about. "The thief comes only to steal and kill and destroy" (John 10:10). But Jesus has a mission, which is told to us in these verses. "I came that they may have life and have it abundantly. I am the good shepherd. The good shepherd lays down his life for the sheep" (John 10:10-11).

So Satan wants to steal, kill and destroy, and Jesus wants to give us life. We get to choose. We are not to blame Satan for everything. Our own foolish hearts and poor choices can also cause us a lot of trouble and pain, too. Much of life is determined by our own choices, whether we will believe Satan and his ways or Jesus and His ways. I say choose Jesus. He overrules Satan every time.

Many books have been written and many sermons preached about suffering. They attempt to answer questions such as, "Why does God allow suffering?" or "If God is loving, why is there so much pain in the world?" or "Why are there starving children in Africa?" We ask, "How come God didn't stop that plane from crashing and keep those innocent people from dying?" and other similar questions.

These are misled questions. The better questions are "Why does God even love us? We are fallen, ignorant, rebellious, and stubborn. Why does He give us a path out of our suffering? Why is He so gracious to provide for us to be forgiven for our sins and wrongs, while we are drowning in our own pride? Why does He choose to heal our brokenness and diseases? Why does He choose to provide us jobs, food, and clothing? Why does He extend His loving hand to us while we ignore Him and use His name as curse words? Why is God so good? *Why does God love us?*"

We have completely misunderstood God and how the world works. The world is filled with people who want to be told they are okay and that with a little patching up their lives will be peaceful, with little or no trouble or heartache. This is not the truth.

When you kids were in grade school and would do something wrong, we would discipline you. None of you wanted this. I remember one instance I had sternly corrected you and sent you to your room. A while later, I came to your room to console you and to try and restore the loving relationship between us. You were mad at me for disciplining you and more mad at yourself for getting caught. You then started to pity yourself and said, "I am so rotten. I was so dumb to do that."

My first instinct was to quickly tell you that you are not rotten, and that you are not dumb but a good and smart girl, while I am worrying about making sure you had a good self-image. No good mother wants her child to spiral down into depression. But what I said to you is, "Yes, your heart is very rotten. We are all born rotten. You are not wise, and you have made a very bad choice. This is why we need a Savior, to save us from ourselves and our own rotten choices."

You blinked and gave me a wide-eyed stare, because you probably thought I would tell you that you are a smart, good girl and join you in your pity party. But we aren't good. It's a lie to tell you that you are basically good. We are not basically good. From birth, we are born with sin natures. No one has to teach a toddler how to lie and to demand her own way. We are bent towards evil until God redeems us through Jesus and we are born again into life in Christ. I did not have to teach any of you kids to lie, hurt each other, and argue with each other. This sin nature is natural, and we are born with it. All you kids were skilled sinners from the beginning. We all are.

But because we are made in the image of God and have immense intrinsic value because of that, we need to be rescued from our fallen natures, our bad choices, and our powerlessness to do anything about them. This is why we need a Savior and why we need redemption. We need Him to save us and give us power over sin, the power to choose what is right. This is the trouble Jesus warned us about, and much of the New Testament tells us what Jesus does for us and how He does it. Jesus Christ is the only way of escape.

Do not be misled and believe the lies of Satan. In this life, you are promised and guaranteed that you will live in a constant state of trouble. Expect it! And then when the relief comes, when the forgiveness is given, when the healing happens, when you are delivered, you can rejoice with a heart overflowing with thankfulness to God.

He delivers us from all of our troubles, but the trouble with trouble is that it keeps coming. In this life we will constantly be plagued with trouble. But God, who is so loving and good, chose to love us and give us those things we need. He provides for us a way of escape and delivers us from pain and misery in the midst of our troubles.

He is the answer. He is such a sweet relief. His gentle touch, His quiet comfort, His steady assurance, His steadfast love, His forgiveness when we ask. He will come and live in you when you ask. He specializes in deliverance and healing. He is our rescue, our very help. He is the sustainer of our lives. He is the lover of our souls. This is who He is and these are what He provides for us in the midst of all this trouble.

"God is our refuge and strength, a very present help in trouble" (Psalm 46:1).

"In your righteousness deliver me and rescue me; incline your ear to me, and save me! (Psalm 71:2).

"Help us, O God of our salvation, for the glory of your name; deliver us, and atone for our sins, for your name's sake!" (Psalm 79:9).

"Remember my affliction and my wanderings, the wormwood and the gall! My soul continually remembers it and is bowed down within me. But this I call to mind, and therefore I have hope: The steadfast love of the Lord never ceases, his mercies never come to an end; they are new every morning; great is your faithfulness.

"The Lord is my portion," says my soul, "therefore I will hope in him. The Lord is good to those who wait for him, to the soul who seeks him. It is good that one should wait quietly for the salvation of the Lord" (Lamentations 3:19-26).

24

Solitude

*S*mart phones beep, ring, vibrate, and chirp amongst us now. Everywhere we go (and that is not an exaggeration) the smart phone dominates what our eyes are fixed on, what we are thinking about, how we walk, and where we go. Dead is the coffee shop or public place that doesn't have Wi-Fi. Smart phones interrupt our conversations and thoughts and give us attention spans of about a millisecond. It's so frustrating to be talking with people and their phones ring or beep. They completely break their eye contacts and their brain engagements and check the phones. If they are rude without an "excuse me" or "pardon me," they then answer the texts or take the calls. Why do phone calls seem more demanding of their attention than talking to the persons in front of them?

Distraction plagues the human brain. So much is going on in our brains at one time that distractions and the inability to focus are natural, the default positions of our thinking. Our brains are naturally useless and idle, and I would argue bent towards evil, unless trained to be used for good. Just like an athlete trains his or her muscles, conditioning and strengthening them to be stronger to attempt to win an athletic competition, so must we train and condition our brains to think usefully and constructively to be successful.

Just when it would be to our benefit to concentrate on something important or go deeper into conversations with others, smart phones buzz or the next links appear on the screens and our thoughts are interrupted. Capturing the moment of meaningful conversations with people or just on the brink of good ideas while we are having time to ourselves, we short-circuit our conversations and our thoughts while we turn our attentions to beeping cell phones and the flashing icons on computer screens. Is it really more important than what we were doing before they buzzed, beeped, or flashed? Some have allowed themselves to be slaves to these little devices.

With this heavy usage of smart phones, especially amongst the younger generation, we are training our brains to live in a world of distraction, with subjects given very little thought or time. The lust of the eyes is never satisfied, and we are fascinated with news and videos, text messages, and social media. Movements and colors on the screens keep us watching but never satisfied enough so we say, "I'm satisfied now, so I can shut it off."

After a good meal at the dinner table, we know we are full, so we stop eating and get up from the table after everyone else has finished eating also. We rarely feel this way in front of screens. Our brains will never say "enough" to where we naturally feel we are "full," and it's time to turn the devices off and leave them. We need to learn to shut them off.

Deeper analysis or concentration is not learned or practiced while we are staring at screens that are entertaining us, and we are not training our brains to think usefully or creatively. This kind of interrupted brain activity does not lend itself to developing longer thought processes necessary to find peace or to solve problems.

First of all, let me say that I did not write this to make you feel guilty because I think your generation, and a lot of mine, spend way too much time in front of screens. Although I'm from a different generation, I realize that to communicate and work these days, smart phones are almost required. Life will be different for you than it has been for me because of hand-held phones. And I know personally that many friendships and relationships have been greatly enriched because of smart phones and personal computers, which allow us to access each other through email and social media sites.

We need to be aware of what they are doing to our brains and discipline ourselves to use them properly. Why this discussion about hand-held phones? I believe they have become one of the biggest enemies of solitude.

When you were a little girl and your brothers were at school and you and I were home for a few hours, you would play with your dolls, paint pictures with watercolors, play the piano, write stories and just generally be content with your bit of solitude. I had trained you to do this.

Starting at toddlerhood, I would put you in your playpen with toys and explain that you had to play in there for a while. This was usually after a busy day when we needed a break and some rejuvenation. The playpen was in the family room so you could see me cleaning up the house or relaxing myself, and I expected you to entertain yourself for a while. At the time, I was doing this more for my benefit than for yours, honestly. Gradually, over time as you grew, I moved you into your bedroom for this daily resting time. Sometimes you fell asleep in your bed, and sometimes you played with your toys and dolls. I would set the timer, and after an hour or so, the timer would ring and you would come out of your room and get back to the busyness that filled each day.

As you grew, and were in grade school and middle school, it was natural for you to go into your room and retreat from everything for a while, even if a lot of busyness and action were going on in the house. This was your solitude: time to think, play, make music, debrief from the day, collect yourself and your thoughts, and enjoy the quiet. I had trained you to want and appreciate solitude because now you felt the effects and benefits of it. As you grow and move away from home, I suggest you make time for solitude each day and give it a place of importance in your life.

Jesus was an excellent example of this. He often withdrew to a solitary place to pray. He would often leave large crowds that needed His touch and healing to withdraw and be alone. If Jesus did this to pray and be alone with His heavenly Father, certainly we need to do this, too.

Even though I trained you to practice solitude, it is something that you must now do on your own and continue to practice as an adult. Just like kids are trained to play sports, if they are to continue in adulthood, they must do it on their own. No longer are Mom and Dad there to make sure that they practice good habits and live healthy lifestyles.

A disclaimer: Each of us requires a different amount of solitude to maintain a healthy brain and lifestyle. Recognize how much you need, and put it on the calendar to schedule some solitude into your day. It may seem selfish or unimportant, but it's not. Give yourself permission to make time for it.

Solitude is something we have to contend for, to plan ahead for, to protect and strive for. It will not happen unless we make it happen, schedule it on the calendar, and practice it. It is a necessary part of our day for each one of us, and some of us need more solitude than others.

Wasted time while we are alone is not solitude. Solitude is intentional time alone for a purpose. Don't forget to turn off your smart phone and the screens around you. By the way, God has already sent you the best text messages, and they are in the Bible. Those short, potent verses say so much.

Solitude is the place to be alone to relax, unwind, debrief ourselves, and pray. Here we can read our Bibles, confess our sins to God, unload our burdens, and find forgiveness. It's time to be creative, use our imaginations for what we want to do or want to be, and to dream. It's time to focus on God, appreciate what He has done for us in the past and realize He will be faithful to us in the future. It's time to connect with Jesus and find Him in the busyness and noise of our lives. It's time to pour praise and thanksgiving back to Him for all He has poured into us. It's time to be still, to stop, to think, to create, to imagine, to suppose.

Forced solitude is often loneliness, and we don't want that. We were made to benefit from solitude, but loneliness hurts us. Loneliness and solitude are very different; they are not the same thing. And through the years, I have planned ahead and trained myself so most of the time I can quickly convert loneliness to solitude. This takes practice and discipline, but it can be done.

In my own experience, it has often been difficult to get to a place where I like solitude. If I am hurt, grieving, angry, tired, lonely, bored, or have unconfessed sins, often solitude looks and feels like torture. During solitude, buried pain often emerges, which we may have worked so hard to avoid. I think that's why a lot of people avoid being alone because it is painful. They do not know how to use alone time or have not realized that it can lead to beneficial solitude and to God, if they allow it. He can really get to the deeper places in our souls and hearts and bless us during our times of solitude, if we allow Him to.

If solitude looks like torture and being alone is something that you work hard to avoid, I challenge you to figure out why you feel this way. Are you avoiding God? Are you sensing the voice of the Holy Spirit that convicts you of sin, and so you feel the guilt because you have wronged God or others? If so, take care of this. Maybe you need to confess your sins to God or to another trusted friend, or ask people you have wronged for their forgiveness. But do whatever needs to be done so you don't run from alone time with God and fear solitude.

In various seasons of my life, I did not want or like solitude, as it meant misery or emptiness. As you know, I lost my closest friend of thirty years to cancer in 2010, and solitude that year was weeping, sadness, and grieving for her. She was the sister I never had. But as God brought me through that season and I didn't avoid Him or the steps He lead me through to get through my grief, I have finally come to understand that solitude is good for me. He is good for me and so very good to all of us.

Now, I crave daily solitude. My appetite for it is immense. If I have been with people or family non-stop for a few days, I can feel myself missing that sweet connection with God that solitude provides. But it took me a long time to get to this place to have the peace of mind so I could enjoy solitude.

So please remember, precious daughter, when you are feeling frazzled, tired, weary, or something is bothering you but you can't quite figure out what, I suggest you make time for solitude so you can debrief yourself. Pour your heart out to God, be honest with Him and yourself, and write your thoughts and prayers in a journal if that helps. It's beneficial to unwind the tension and finally get quiet enough to hear what the Lord is saying to you. And as you mature and go through many seasons, hopefully you will build solitude into your day. He is always speaking. Are we listening?

"Be still before the Lord and wait patiently for him" (Psalm 37:7).

"And leaving them, he went out of the city to Bethany and lodged there. In the morning, as he was returning to the city" (Matthew 21:17-18).

"Now when Jesus heard this, he withdrew from there in a boat to a desolate place by himself" (Matthew 14:13).

25

Don't Rush This

*Y*ou got your driver's license today. We came home together from the driver's license office, and you were beaming. You quickly jumped in the old pickup, which both of your brothers learned to drive in, and now the keys are yours. You're driving around town, somewhere, any-where, freedom flowing in your veins, and the wind blowing in your hair.

I remember the day we brought you home from the hospital as a newborn, wrapped in a couple of blankets and strapped into the car seat. Now you are driving a vehicle yourself. Where did the time go?

And I remember your dad running behind your bicycle when you were little, holding the back of the seat just after he took the training wheels off, making sure you would stay upright and not fall off your bike. Now you're driving a vehicle. Where did the time go?

I feel the passage of time so keenly because you are my only girl and our last born. I am trying not to be so stunned that this much time has gone by. Life goes by really, really fast, at breakneck speed. The Bible says our lives are but a mist. This isn't a statement of our value but of how short time is for us here on earth.

Throughout my life I have waited for the next thing, talked about it, and planned for it. *I can't wait until I get my driver's license. I can't wait until I graduate from high school. I can't wait until I graduate from college. I want to get married. When am I going to have kids? When are these kids finally going to be potty trained? I can't wait until these kids are in school, then I'll have time for myself. I can't wait until these kids grow up, and I'll have less work to do,* and on and on I told myself.

I now have more gray hair than brown, more wrinkles with each passing month, brown spots on the backs of my hands, a sore back and neck, and need reading glasses. This passage of time has gone very fast.

I have accomplished a lot. I have covered a lot of miles, been many places, and seen a lot. But I wish someone had told me, *don't rush this.*

Take time to enjoy each stage. You will arrive at the next stage soon enough. Force yourself to pause, make yourself slow down, enjoy the moment, and give thanks to God for all He has given you at every stage every day.

Stop and reflect on what God has done. Write it down, take photos and recollect how wonderful life is, how blessed we are, and how much God loves us. Enjoy every stage and every day.

Don't rush through it, wishing for the weekend, the next big event, the next vacation, the next phase. It will come. Stop and capture the time, the blessings, the good that God has given you. Don't just gloss over the good in each day, the kindness of friends, the beauty of the outdoors, the changing of the seasons, the satisfaction of a good meal, the comfort of a warm cup of tea. Be thankful for your family that loves you, your friends that surround you, and those in your life who have taught you something and given themselves to you in doing so. Appreciate those who are older than you and have experienced a lot more life than you have, and tell them why you appreciate them.

Notice beauty. Seek peace and happiness and pursue them. Hug your family and friends. Stop and take extra time to listen to someone who needs an ear. Give lavishly, even if it hurts. Open your heart wider to others. Go out of your way to do something good for someone else, expecting nothing in return. Give your time, talents, and money to those who can never repay you. Donate time and money anonymously. Pray for those who will never know you did so. And pray for others and tell them. Pray with your family and good friends often. Go to a bible-preaching church every week. Do the important more than you do the urgent. Tell God often what you are thankful for, and tell others when you are thankful for them.

Make it a priority each day to remember the good, your salvation, your redemption, your inheritance in the kingdom. Figure out a way and intentionally mark time. Discipline yourself to slow down and enjoy the time.

Be thankful to God for what you have. The years fly by. The days are long and the years are short. Forgive others often. Love lavishly. Enjoy your youth while you have it. It will fade quickly. Be the one who notices those who are not noticed. Reach out to others who are in pain. Help the down-trodden, and encourage the weak. Remember the good. Remember to enjoy life.

Value your family, your friends, and your church. Value what God values. Keep your eyes in the Good Book daily. The things that are so good, yet unseen, are eternal.

Rejoice for what God has given you, and constantly give thanks to Him. Pause each day to realize what you have.

Don't rush this.

"Come now, you who say, 'Today or tomorrow we will go to into such and such a town and spend a year there and trade and make a profit' — yet you do not know what tomorrow will bring. What is your life? For you are a mist that appears for a little time and then vanishes. Instead you ought to say, 'If the Lord wills, we will live and do this or that' " (James 4:13-15).

"Rejoice in the Lord always; again I will say, Rejoice. Let your reasonableness be known to everyone. The Lord is at hand; do not be anxious about anything, but in everything by prayer and supplication with thanksgiving let your requests be made known to God. And the peace of God, which surpasses all understanding, will guard your hearts and your minds in Christ Jesus" (Philippians 4:4-7).

26

Love

" *L*ove is patient and kind; love does not envy or boast; it is not arrogant or rude. It does not insist on its own way; it is not irritable or resentful; it does not rejoice at wrongdoing, but rejoices with the truth. Love bears all things, believes all things, hopes all things, endures all things.

Love never ends...So now faith, hope and love abide, these three; but the greatest of these is love" (1 Corinthians 13:4-8, 13).

Dear daughter, let's talk about love in this crazy culture that has lost sight of real love. As I read it over, this amazing description of love, I realized again that it is very hard to love like the Bible describes. Well, not very hard but impossible!

Love is completely selfless, always puts others first, has an immense amount of patience, and rejoices, protects, trusts, hopes, and perseveres. It is action.

I love this description of love. It's clear, obvious, to the point, and refreshingly distinct, clearing the fog of what love is and is not. Love is not a feeling, good intentions, or mushy sentiments, although it can be accompanied by those things. Love is action, deeds, work, and choices.

We are told in our culture that we can "fall" in and out of love, this fleeting feeling, often thought to be a euphoric impulse to be caught if "luck" sees fit to have it be ours, and that we can be "lucky in love." Sappy songs, movies, TV, the internet, fashion and gossip magazines, and social media have their definitions of love, and they are always wrong unless they portray the biblical definition of love.

What is love, anyway? We are so confused. So often what is falsely described as love is lust— the opposite of love. Lust is completely self-centered. Lust is impatient, mean, controlling, envious, boastful, and proud. Lust is rude, self-seeking, easily angered, and keeps a long list of wrongs. It's happy about evil: in fact, it celebrates evil. Lust is showy, brazen, and in your face. Lust robs and takes. Many a lustful guy who has gotten a girl to bed quickly discards her and boasts and brags about his conquest. This is pure lust.

Lust does not protect, but it abandons. It does not trust, but it breaks trust and betrays, kills hope, and quickly burns out. Lust always fails and will not last nor sustain a relationship.

My prayer for you is that you will clearly know the difference between love and lust and not be mislead by the noisy messages that our culture say is love but is really lust in disguise.

Sometimes it is difficult at first glance to know the difference between love and lust. Satan, the master of disguise and father of lies, can often fool us and make it hard for us to discern what is love and what is lust. I often am initially confused myself, and when testing my own motives, I have wondered if I am acting out of love or if I am just manipulating the situation to get what I want, lusting after what I should not have.

So, to discern the truth in the midst of the fog, put it to the scriptural test and compare it to 1 Corinthians 13. Here's a list of questions to ask ourselves:

- If I am loving, am I patient, and can what I want wait? Even if I am hungry, tired, and needing sleep, I have learned it is best to be patient, not act impulsively, and to not say things I will later regret.
- Am I kind? This is not being nice. Kindness always has pure motives followed by actions. Being nice (often a close cousin to flattery) can just shroud evil intentions.
- Am I envious and wanting what others have? Am I envying their clothes, possessions, homes, relationships, free time? Or am I content with what I have?

- Am I boastful, making sure others are noticing me, giving me credit and the attention I don't need or deserve? An example for your generation: Posting dozens of photos of themselves on social media, and then girls monitoring the "likes" to see how popular they imagine themselves to be is a classic example of boasting. A few photos on social media are fine, but dozens? It screams self.

- Have I extended kindness, or have I been rude, either in action or tone of voice? How to measure kindness: after you have had encounters or conversations with people, do you think they feel better or worse for having them?

- Am I self-seeking, or do I put myself aside so someone else can get the thanks and the credit? Am I happy for someone else who is recognized or gets recognition for work well done, or am frustrated I didn't get it? God humbles me so much in this area, and over time I have realized His love and care for me, regardless of the amount of outward recognition I receive. Note: An award for humility is one that is never handed out.

- Am I easily angered, or do I practice patience, even when someone is stepping on my last nerve and challenging my patience?

- Do I keep a long list in my head of wrongs committed against me, or do I work hard to forgive and not rehearse the wrongs that have been done to me?

- Do I protect others and their reputations, even if they don't deserve it? Do I fight the urge to expose their weaknesses or stupidity, taking it upon myself to right the wrong, and in doing so, to hurt them back? Do I guard my tongue against gossip to protect someone else's feelings and reputation?

- Am I trusting God, hoping, and persevering? Or am I giving up easily when it gets hard, or when I am impatient and would rather just give in?

I know this list is a tall order. I fail daily. No one is perfect. That is why we need a Savior.

God is love. He is perfect love. Even though I am over half a century old, this still intrigues me, blesses me, humbles me, and lifts me. We have not even begun to scratch the surface of God's love for us. Why does He love such sinful, dirty, dumb, fallen, messed up, broken people as we all are? Why? Why does He choose to love us? How can such a holy God love us? I do not understand it, but I thoroughly need His love.

"He heals the brokenhearted and binds up their wounds" (Psalm 147:3).

"A bruised reed he will not break, and a smoldering wick he will not snuff out" (Isaiah 42:3 NIV).

"Beloved, let us love one another, for love is from God, and whoever loves has been born of God and knows God. Anyone who does not love does not know God, because God is love. In this the love of God was made manifest among us, that God sent his only Son into the world, that we might live through him. In this is love, not that we loved God, but that he loved us and sent his Son to be the propitiation for our sins. Beloved, if God so loved us, we also ought to love one another. No one has ever seen God; if we love one another, God abides in us and his love is perfected in us" (1 John 4:7-12).

"God is love, and whoever abides in love abides in God, and God abides in him. By this is love perfected with us, so that we may have confidence for the day of judgment, because as he is so also are we in this world. There is no fear in love, but perfect love casts out fear. For fear has to do with punishment, and whoever fears is not been perfected in love. We love because he first loved us... And this commandment we have from him: whoever loves God must also love his brother" (1 John 4:16-19, 21).

27

Final Thoughts to My Daughter

As I think about this book, all I have written to you, all I want for you, all I dream for you, I give it to you with much joy in my heart. I am proud of you and the choices you have made in your life.

Yes, we have had our rough times when you were seething mad at me because as your mother I didn't let you do what you shouldn't do or go where you shouldn't go. My job as your mother is to protect, teach, encourage, and guide you. And I have done that with the strength the Lord has provided to me after the thousands of times I have asked Him, often knowing you would be very angry at me and shut me out of your room and heart. But I decided long ago that I am going to be your mother, and in time I realized that we would eventually also become friends. Yes, now we are friends!

We have had more than twenty years together that the Lord has given us. He has given me so much joy and healing because of you. Seeing how your dad, the love of my life and the man the Lord has given me, loves you, cares for you, takes time to talk to you, hugs you, spends time with you, texts you and calls you has been such a great example of how the heavenly Father loves and acts towards us, His daughters.

So I've edited this book that I gave to you on your high school graduation day, revised it, added to it, and written additional letters realizing it will be read by more women than just you.

Thank you for allowing me to share our story with so many. I hope you will benefit even further from it and continue to be a light and a living example amongst the women in your generation.

You are an amazing young woman and have much joy, potential, love, and compassion. I am humbled and honored to be your mother, and I wait expectantly to see how God is going to unfold your life.

Text me.

All my love and devotion,

Mom

xxxooo

28

To Other Daughters Besides My Own

*N*ow you've read the letters to my daughter, my deep desires for her, lessons to her, my heart for her. I've allowed you to see a bit into our lives. I have a heart for daughters who are not my own but whom I care about deeply. I know some will appreciate and benefit from what I have said, and some will disagree with and rebuff what I have said. Just the word mother triggers a strong reaction in us, regardless of how we were mothered.

I know many women, regardless of their age, were not mothered well. Many were never taught what they needed to know about life. Many women have arrived at motherhood themselves, bruised and broken, realizing they now have sons or daughters that need whole, emotionally-well mothers, and they aren't.

Many girls and women have been abandoned, neglected, mistreated, ignored, pushed aside, shamed, punished, emotionally abused, manipulated, and hurt in many other ways by mothers who were supposed to love and care for them. Or their mothers stood by and watched these things being done to them by others, and they did nothing to stop it.

Reading this book, some women will be in a lot of pain, realizing that they have deep, bleeding wounds inside or scars that cover so much of their souls that their hearts can't feel much anymore. When we have been in a very dark room for a long time or asleep throughout the night, when a light is suddenly flicked on, our eyes hurt, and we cannot see anything until they adjust. This is what reading this book may be like. Eventually, eyes adjust, and they can see well when the light comes on. I hope over time eyes will adjust, and guided by the loving hand of our heavenly Father, daughters will eventually be all right.

I have argued with God and hesitated so many times about putting all of this in book form, printing copies, making it available electronically, and distributing it so others could read these things I spent ten years writing to my daughter. First, because these letters are so personal, and second, because the things stated here are so far away from the norm in our culture and from what most women have been taught today. I get it.

But after much thought, prayer, preparation, and wrestling, I cast the fear aside and print my heart on paper for my daughter and for others willing to read my words. I hope it blesses you.

Most of all, know that Jesus loves you. This may sound trite or ridiculous, but it's true. Some of us have heard this in our childhoods or read it on posters at football games, listened to a Christian tell her story, heard it while randomly flipping through radio stations, or heard it in church. It's true; it really is true.

It is my prayer that you will understand the full meaning of who we are as humans, why God made us, and what this is all for, anyway. Over time, I hope you come to know and follow the Savior who so deeply loves us and is the only One who can heal us.

I also hope this book can be a conversation starter for you and your own daughter, possibly reading it together (if it is age appropriate). I hope it helps you figure out some of the topics you may want to talk to her about.

If you are a young girl or woman reading this book and wish you had a mother who would have taught you these things, I understand. Maybe a life goal for you would be to seek God for the grace and healing you need and then resolve to teach these things to other young women, and your daughter one day, should you be blessed to have one.

Please contact me or visit my blog. I will not have many of the answers, but maybe I can fill in and be your mother for a few minutes, listening and being there with words.

My blog is MotherhoodMatters.org.

You may contact me there.

About the Author

*J*anis Kristiansen was born in Seattle and raised in Washington State. She is married to her husband of over thirty years, Washington State Representative Dan Kristiansen, who serves in the legislature as the Washington State House Minority Leader.

They have two grown sons, a daughter-in-law, and a daughter in college. They also helped raise a third "son" as they call him, starting when he was in high school.

Janis has served in various capacities, helping women for years; in Mothers of Preschoolers (MOPS) when her kids were young, for a few years as a pre-marriage counselor with her husband, and as Family Life group leaders in two churches. She currently is a small group leader of a high school girls' bible study, and serves as a MOPS mentor.

She has a bachelor of science degree in the College of Forestry from the University of Washington. For her professional career, she is the Vice President and environmental coordinator for a manufacturing firm and serves on the regulatory affairs committee for the trade association involving the industry.

Marriage and motherhood are two subjects she has spent a lot of time learning and writing about. Helping girls and women navigate these issues is her passion.

She may be contacted through her blog: MotherhoodMatters.org.

Your own thoughts to your daughter, another young girl,
or your younger self

Your own thoughts to your daughter, another young girl, or your younger self

Your own thoughts to your daughter, another young girl,
or your younger self

*Your own thoughts to your daughter, another young girl,
or your younger self*

Your own thoughts to your daughter, another young girl,
or your younger self

CPSIA information can be obtained
at www.ICGtesting.com
Printed in the USA
FSOW03n0952070218
44271FS